THE UNITED STATES
IN THE CHANGING
GLOBAL ECONOMY

THE UNITED STATES
IN THE CHANGING
GLOBAL ECONOMY

Policy Implications and Issues

GEORGE MACESICH

Westport, Connecticut
London

Library of Congress Cataloging-in-Publication Data

Macesich, George, 1927–
    The United States in the changing global economy : policy
implications and issues / George Macesich.
        p.   cm.
    Includes bibliographical references and index.
    ISBN 0–275–95705–5 (alk. paper)
        1. United States—Economic conditions—1981–   2. United States—
Economic policy—1993–   3. United States—Foreign economic
relations.   I. Title.
    HC106.82   1997
    330.973′0927—dc20   96–44686

British Library Cataloguing in Publication Data is available.

Library of Congress Catalog Card Number: 96–44686
ISBN: 0–275–95705–5

First published in 1997

Praeger Publishers, 88 Post Road West, Westport, CT 06881
An imprint of Greenwood Publishing Group, Inc.

Printed in the United States of America

The paper used in this book complies with the
Permanent Paper Standard issued by the National
Information Standards Organization (Z39.48–1984).

10 9 8 7 6 5 4 3 2 1

Contents

Preface

As we approach the 21st century, it is clear that the accelerating globalization of world markets and increasing interdependence of the world's economies have made policy making very complex indeed. This is particularly the case for the United States, which is still the world's largest and most important economy. In fact, one of the most debated subjects in recent years was whether the United States was capable of simultaneously dealing with serious domestic challenges and growing globalization of the world economy. These issues were a focal point in recent American presidential elections.

Perceived and actual problems that the Untied States has experienced in recent years are underscored in such issues as economic instability and unemployment, particularly among white-collar workers. In fact, real wages for most Americans have not increased much over the last twenty years. There is a feeling of discontent that much is wrong in America and that change is necessary if it is to be competitive in a growing global economy. In particular, American secondary education is faulted because it is believed that students simply are not prepared to compete against American rivals in the global marketplace. The international debt status of America is an ongoing source of concern.

This book discusses the accelerating global economy and its implications for policy. The impact of these changes for the American economy and policy is discussed at length. The book draws on and weaves together institutional, theoretical, and empirical results and policy analysis so that each reinforces the other. Only when many strands are woven together can we have a useful understanding of issues as complex as those involving the American economy. The book is directed to the general economist, political scientist, and layperson. It is particularly important that nonspecialists understand the issues confronting the American economy in a period of rapid acceleration of the global economy.

I am indebted to many colleagues with whom I have discussed one or another aspect of this book over the years. These include Marshall R. Colberg, Walter Macesich, Jr., Milton Friedman, and Anna J. Schwartz.

Chapter 1

The Changing Global Economy

INTEGRATING THE GLOBAL ECONOMY

For all the starts and stops, the world continues on a course of integration that began in the post–World War II years. Indeed, the wave of worldwide integration that started soon after the war has had more powerful and beneficial effects than the much more advertised and talked about series of regional integration.[1] In fact, according to Haberler, there was fear that attempts at regional integration in various parts of the world constitute an eminent danger to worldwide integration and further growth of multilateral trade.

Haberler pointed out that such regional integration as the EEC (formerly the European Economic Cooperation and now the European Community) are viewed by some as a step toward freer trade. Good intentions, however, are not enough. An international enterprise of the magnitude of the EEC, he observed, once it has been launched and institutionalized through the creation of a heavy politico-bureaucratic machinery, tends to develop its own logic and movement. After it has gathered momentum, it becomes very difficult to steer it in another direction.

Haberler's observation made in the mid-1960s is valid today. This has been discovered, to their sorrow, by many people who have been trying to persuade the Europeans to adopt an outward-looking attitude, particularly toward East Europeans and others. It may still be too early to say of the European Community, as Alfred Marshall said of the German *Zollverein*, that it was a big step toward freer multilateral trade.

Haberler also observed that future growth of world trade and even closer integration of the major areas of the world will depend on two conditions. The first and basic requirement is maintenance of a high level of employment and growth in the industrial countries. The second is further liberalization of trade or, as a minimum, avoidance of increases in trade barriers for balance-of-payments or protectionist reasons. We cannot be as sure of the second condition as we can of the first because balance-of-payments problems among industrial countries could easily become a serious roadblock to freer trade.

By integration we take Haberler's definition to mean closer economic relations between areas concerned.[2] Clearly it is a concept capable of continuous gradation. Characteristically, the first state of integration is the tendency toward equalization of commodity prices through free commodity trade and greater division of labor. A higher stage of integration occurs when factors of production can move freely with a consequent tendency for factor price equalization. We have, as Haberler notes, a still higher stage of integration if "all or most important phases of economic policy are coordinated, and positive steps taken to equalize commodity and factor prices."[3]

The various integration movements on the current world scene can be viewed as manifestations of more fundamental waves of worldwide economic integration. In fact, Haberler argues that in the past two hundred years or so, we can identify three big waves of integration that in many respects dwarf postwar attempts at regional integration. This secular trend toward worldwide integration, he observes, was interrupted by one period of sharp decline and disintegration.

In this view, the first wave can be identified as the internal integration of the economies of nation-states. The first national economy so integrated was that of Great Britain, followed by the French and American economies. Subsequently came the economies of other European and overseas countries.

Superimposed on the first wave is a second one characterized by the free trade movement, which reached a high point at the end of the 1870s. The movement was reversed in 1878 by imposition in most countries of even higher tariffs. Nevertheless, world trade continued to grow rapidly up to World War I, due in good measure to rapid technological advances and large migration of both labor and capital toward regions of relatively recent settlement, such as the Americas. At the same time, instruments of the modern state, such as economic planning, quotas, and other interventionist methods, had not reached the level of contemporary sophistication.

The rising protectionism and nationalism from 1880 onward foreshadowed the collapse in worldwide economic integration during and in the immediate post–World War I period. A brief revival in free trade and the secular trend toward integration in the 1920s then collapsed with the Great Depression. Thereafter, real disintegration and rapid decline of world trade set in and reached a low point during World War II.

The third wave of worldwide integration and growth started soon after World War II and picked up momentum in the 1950s and 1960s. The impressive postwar recovery of the major industrial countries ultimately spread worldwide and served to set off the third worldwide wave of economic integration that Haberler discusses.

With the collapse of the Soviet Union and other socialist states and their subsequent, if successful, transition to market economies, we may have the beginning of a fourth wave of worldwide integration as important as the other three. Certainly, the likelihood that the United States and other countries will incorporate the General Agreement on Tariffs and Trade (GATT) into their trade relations promises to give momentum to this growth wave of international economic integration. This global trade pact initiated in the spring of 1994 by more than one hundred nations reportedly could generate $5 trillion in new worldwide commerce by the year 2005.

Alhough it is not perfect, GATT does reduce import tariffs worldwide by an average of 40 percent and covers areas of concern for such countries as the United States in agriculture, intellectual property, and some services. As a result, these tariff reductions will surely stimulate worldwide trade, create more jobs, and lead to greater prosperity. They will almost certainly speed up the processes of worldwide integration.

Attempts at strengthening and accelerating the current wave of world integration can be seen in the sphere of international money and finance and, in particular, in the world's capital markets.[4] Rohatyn puts it well: Despite threats and conflicts within different regimes of the world, growth of worldwide capital markets has gone ahead relentlessly. A legitimate worldwide market in stocks, bonds, currencies, and other financial instruments has emerged, tied together by modern data processing and communications technology and operating twenty-four hours a day.[5] Indeed, it is variously estimated that between 1990 and 2020 the output of the G-7 "rich countries" will grow from $13 to $24 trillion during the period for an average growth rate of less than 2 percent a year. The output of the "nonrich" countries—for example, China, India, Indonesia, and Russia—is expected to grow from $9 trillion to over $34 trillion over the same period, or at about 4.5 percent per year.

Assuming, for the sake of argument, that these estimates are reasonable, argue amounts of capital will be required to sustain such growth. Global competition for capital will likely concentrate the attention of countries in need of capital on making economic and political reforms likely to encourage the mobilization of domestic and foreign savings. If they are to tap into private investment, these countries must push ahead with reforms aimed at a stable currency, receptive social and political institutions, and, of course, a growing economy.

Given the magnitude and risks involved, it is with good reason that Rohatyn suggests the adoption of worldwide investment standards. He argues that there should be a separate and comprehensive organization comparable to GATT for investment just as there is GATT for trade, even though some aspects of invest-ment are covered under GATT.[6] If such arrangements are in place, it is likely that Western investors, including pension funds, insurance funds, mutual funds, and others with fiduciary responsibilities, will look with added interest into foreign investment.

Other countries also fall far short of guaranteeing international investors the kinds of protection now given to American securities legislation. For instance, the European Community has made attempts in this direction and encouraged regulation to protect investors. How far such efforts have to go is suggested in the case of Germany, where as late as 1994 legislation was introduced requiring higher disclosure standards, more adequate protection for minority shareholders, and severe penalties for insider trading. In fact, in 1994 Daimler-Benz was the only major German company to adopt the accounting standards that have been a basic requirement of American securities laws for years if a firm is to be listed on the New York Stock Exchange.

It is thus with good reason that an appropriate model may well be the American capital market. The legal protections; the requirement of disclosure; the variety of financial instruments available to investors, including stocks, bonds, mutual funds, options, and futures; the technical capacities of the system—all suggest standards singularly lacking in many countries. They will, however, be required if local capital markets are to be connected in a satisfactory manner with global capital markets. In any case, the capital necessary to finance reasonable rates of worldwide is simply beyond the capacities of the West, either from public or private funds. World growth thus requires efficient and effective capital markets in all countries to provide for and sustain the fourth wave of international integration. Again, the 1994–95 financial problems of Mexico serve to underscore the likely development of future events. Flexible or floating exchange rates would serve international integration.[7]

To a significant extent, the integration the world has achieved in some fifty years since the end of World War II is simply a return to the lack of integration that existed in 1914 at the start of World War I. The financial and monetary ties in 1995, for instance, were still not as impressive as those of pre-1914 years when compared to the size of the economies involved. During the four decades preceding World War I, for example, the British invested a quarter of their savings overseas, mainly in railroads and mines in their colonies and the United States. By contrast, Japanese companies and individuals created fears in the United States that they were "buying America" when they invested 10 percent of their savings outside Japan during the 1980s.

American legislation in 1995 permitted commercial banks, securities firms, and insurance companies to merge with each other and with foreign financial companies. The goal was to make America's financial organizations more competitive in the world. Before 1914, such arrangements were commonplace. Currencies were convertible into gold and thus enabled financial organizations to move money among banking, securities, and industrial ventures worldwide.

Whether successful worldwide economic growth and economic integration is the best way humankind has found to produce stability remains an open issue. Indeed, the argument is all too familiar. British author Sir Norman Angell wrote in 1910 that a European war was impossible because the economies of the world's leading countries had become so interdependent. Four years later, World War I broke out.

IN SEARCH OF STABILITY AND SECURITY

In the immediate post–World War I years, when President Woodrow Wilson addressed the French National Assembly, he brought with him a lofty vision of a new world order. But it was quickly doomed to failure.

Most observers attribute the failure of President Wilson's program to his Republican opponents, who pushed for a return to "normalcy," which led to an American retreat into isolationism. Other observers would also add the failure on Europe's part to stand up to the spread of totalitarianism in the post–World War I era.

In 1994, when President Bill Clinton became the second American leader to address the French parliamentaries, he sketched a vision of a post–Cold War Europe based on transnational integration, security cooperation, the development of free markets, and democracy.

Unfortunately, there are echoes of 1919 in the late-twentieth-century world. Americans appear less than enthusiastic for additional worldwide undertakings, and Europe, for its part, does not seem as confident as it once was in the kind of integration President Clinton envisioned. Once again, Europe is struggling with the resurgence of the kind of right-wing nationalism that led to World War II.

Finally, the tragedy of Yugoslavia underscored the failure of Europe and the United States to achieve common security policies for the post–Cold War era. Premature recognition by a newly reunited Germany of breakaway republics of Yugoslavia within their communist-established administrative frontiers and German pressure on other members of the European Community to do the same certainly do not inspire confidence in future security arrangements.

American management in future European security arrangements may be of the limited sort encapsulated in the Partnership for Peace concept, in which East European states are given a form of cooperation but not membership in the North Atlantic Treaty Organization (NATO). With Russia in the Partnership, the several members can more easily keep watch on each other. These arrangements are not likely to satisfy all parties. A number of the former socialist countries insist on NATO membership.

Much of the concern over NATO and criticism of Russia as the heir of Soviet crimes tends to deny its legitimate security concerns. Indeed, many of Russia's critics apparently are unaware that Poland and Hungary have a history of aggression against Russia and other states. Moreover, Russia was instrumental in dismantling the Soviet system, which was, after all, run by a multiethnic group of political elitists. Russia continues (as of this writing) to recognize and respect the independence of the former Soviet republics, although some of them have lands historically Russian in character.

As for Russia's relationship with the United States and its threat to the West, observers note that Russia was on the Allied side in both world wars. Germany, Japan, and Turkey were not. Russia is now once again able to assume its traditional role with the West. Surely, a security arrangement that does not exclude Russia or other former Warsaw Pact countries is the more desirable approach.

The 1994 European elections for a European Parliament demonstrated to many observers a considerably diminished enthusiasm for pulling together and forging an integrated Europe. To these developments may be added British Prime Minister John Major's desperate attempt, according to some observers, to hold onto the votes of anti-Europeans in his Conservative Party and his abandonment of his last pretense of being a committed European.

Prime Minister Major, who wanted Britain to be at the heart of Europe, has apparently retreated from any such idea. In Major's view, just as desirable would be a multispeed, multi-rack, multilegal Europe—the antithesis of an integrationist vision. In this view of Europe, nations would not merely proceed to unity on different timetables, but some of them would head off in another direction.

The web of problems confronting Europe and the United States in the closing years of the twentieth century include the United States' relationship with Russia, Russia's relationship with the other components of the former Soviet Union, ethnic conflict, racism, the urgent need for economic development of Eastern Europe, chronic Western unemployment and its social consequences, and the tragedy of Yugoslavia. All of these promise to tax the talents of even the most intelligent and stalwart leadership.

Consider, for instance, that several years after the fall of communism and of twenty-two states in central eastern Europe and the former Soviet Union, there are only five countries in which former communists do not hold power or significantly share in governance. Certainly, people do change. Indeed, many of the former communists are viewed as pragmatic, go-slow reformers committed to playing by the rules of the market and democracy. Needless to say, not everyone shares such a view. They point out that the former communists now feel much more self-assured and emboldened by the fact that many of the million who voted for them did so out of hope for a more secure economic and social life, even if the price may well be a return to a good dose of the old order of society.

Transition to market economies and democracy is a difficult process.[8] Certainly, not everyone in the former socialist countries views such a transition as desirable in any case. Millions of industrial workers and pensioners witnessed their jobs and pensions melt away under initial market reforms. They could be expected to vote for the old guard.

Other reasons come to mind rapidly. The spiritual, psychological, and material damage of years under a tightly controlled system are manifest. The sense of self-help, voluntarism, and cooperation in the population has, for the most part, evaporated, due to the all-powerful state and party. Moreover, the *nomenklature* in the former socialist countries has never really relinquished influence over politics and economics.

The fumbling attempts at privatization in these countries has provided the former communists much of the power and influence over the process of privatization. The rampant corruption that has ensued cast in doubt the market reforms themselves. Even when the former communists did lose much party property, their long-established sociopolitical networks remained intact.

The idea that the integration of the former socialist countries with the rest of the world would be a straight shot has misfired. The European Community has not been forthcoming in allowing access to its markets. Indeed, the European Community has increased its protectionist stance toward these countries, further complicating their attempts at reform.

Many of the former socialist countries have turned off political international support by their adoption of a primitive nationalism based on ethnic hatred and xenophobia. Other observers rise in defense of nationalism and religious revival as central to the fragile rebirth of civil society. In any case, nationalism and religious fervor have more often than not served the interests of the former communists and other zealots, as the tragedy of Yugoslavia illustrates. Certainly, nationalism in the former socialist countries has thus far poorly served the creation of a civil society and market democracy. Indeed, the experience in these countries suggests that it is little more than a dangerous threat to stability.

On the other hand, the ex-communists can take little comfort in their revival. There simply can be no return to the old ways of doing business. New constraints are now in place. A growing middle class in these countries and increased trade links with the rest of the world and participation in the worldwide process of integration promise to constrain even the most cynical ex-communist.

The market economy in these countries faces other threats. One is simply the view that property, and particularly private property, is little more than theft. In many of these countries it often is. Many of the new rich have made their money either by stealing state property and calling it "spontaneous privatization," or by bribing an official to give them a license to corner some market. This has served to cast doubt on the honest along with the dishonest and thus undermine the basic sense of fairness of a market economy.

Another threat is the failure in many of these countries to have in place a credible stabilization program. In part, this is due to the lack of a stable monetary and financial organization as well as government will and ability to provide the country with such an organization.

Still another threat is the failure to define the role of the state in postcommunist period. In many of these countries, the state still attempts to provide everything. As a result, it does nothing well. Its tax revenues are drained in support of uneconomic enterprises. Little support for reforms can be expected from the state. Another threat is the lack of a rule of law in these countries. Whatever their merit, laws passed by newly minted parliaments are inadequate if those laws are to be carried out by an unreformed judiciary and police organizations. These are organizations singularly difficult to reform, due to the powerful vested interest they represent.

Despite the problems in these countries, we should bear in mind that at the end of World War II it took most of Europe more than twenty years to achieve freely convertible currencies and a reasonably stable political environment. In effect, it took almost a generation, notwithstanding the large amount of aid provided to Europe by the American Marshall Plan and the European experience with market economies. All of this was much easier politically and economically than the tasks currently facing the world's former socialist countries.

AN AMERICAN ROLE: A NOTE OF CAUTION

Many an observer has urged Americans to curb their missionary zeal in dealing with other peoples and countries. This is particularly the case, they argue, in the American prescription to many emerging countries to establish multiparty systems as quickly as possible. The more likely result, in this view, is chaos rather than democracy. In a world torn by struggling nationalist governments and ethnic rivalries, caution in extending advice may be the correct watchword.

For reasons that are now becoming increasingly clear, the end of the Cold War, multiparty democracy, and respect for human rights have not spread as rapidly as many Americans and other observers had expected. In Rwanda, for example, the establishment of a multiparty system and a coalition government in 1992 hardened ethnic division, which erupted into civil war and genocide in 1994. In Cambodia, the United Nations spent several billion dollars on a high-profile election in 1993 that has provided an increasingly dictatorial, corrupt, and brutal government that cannot even control its army. In Haiti, one can only hope that the regime of Jean-Bertrand Aristide can keep the country together with American assistance.

It may well be that American support for democracy abroad should be directed, as some analysts urge, to countries that already have an established bureaucracy and a middle class that pays income tax and in which the main issues of property and power sharing have been resolved, leaving politicians to argue about budgets. In their view, democratic elections often intensify ethnic and regional divisions rather than heal them. Thus in the Caucasus, the collapse of the Soviet Union brought nationalist-democrats to power in Armenia and Azerbajian. Each leader furthered his country's slide into a brutal war against the other. Indeed, it was only later, with the removal from power of the freely elected president of Azerbajian by former communists that a modicum of stability returned and a cease-fire between the two countries went into effect.

The sorry spectacle of Yugoslavia is but another example of "free" elections bringing to power nationalist-democrats who promptly created disaster for all concerned. Authoritarian regimes may well be odious to many Americans and so compel them to become involved in the internal affairs of another country. Again, caution may be the wiser course of action than to choose sides, as in the three-sided civil war in Yugoslavia.

There are lessons that we should avoid more Yugoslavias. Many of the same politicians and diplomats who shaped the history through their own errors and failures are still in office (as of 1996). The warning to go slow in the recognition of Yugoslavia's secessionist republics was not heeded. The result was war and the sending of American ground forces to keep a tenuous peace in the region.

One lesson is certainly underscored: Do not recognize a new country without first finding out if the proposed government is in fact in control of the territory it claims. The Bosnian Muslims, for instance, came to count on outside help to establish control of the secessionist Bosnia. This ultimately resulted in the sending of American and NATO ground forces.

Another lesson is that a people who want independence must make concessions that will persuade other powerful ethnic or nationality groups to live in the same country, let them go, or be prepared to fight without the benefit of external assistance and/or sponsorship.

Still another lesson, especially for Americans, is to brush aside the soothing assurances of politicians, diplomats, journalists, and so-called military experts that the use of air power will not lead to the introduction of ground forces. As experience in Bosnia once again illustrates, use of air power does indeed lead to the use of ground power.

To compound the potential for disaster, the United States has not only committed its ground troops to keeping a tenuous peace in Bosnia, but also to arming and training the Bosnian Muslims in order to create a stable balance of power—so the United States will eventually be able to leave. How does the United States intend to be a passive, neutral peacekeeper between Serbs, Croats, and Muslims with one hand, while arming and training the Muslims with the other?

For what it is worth, Americans have now learned that NATO has changed. Apparently the organization is no longer supposed to bind its members to mutual protection against attack, but others as well. Not everyone in the United States is satisfied with the change, nor with the failure on the part of American policy makers to spell out the consequences.

The fact is that from the beginning of the wars in Yugoslavia in 1991, the European Community (EC) was running all of the diplomacy in Yugoslavia and had organized a peace conference in search of a comprehensive settlement among the participants in the conflict. The guiding principle was that the EC would not give diplomatic recognition to any breakaway republics of Yugoslavia (which began with Croatia and Slovenia pulling out in 1991) unless and until they agreed to peace accords between them and guaranteed the rights of other ethnic and/or national groups.

Acting on their own, the Germans, led by their Foreign Minister Hans-Deitrich Genscher, told the EC that Germany would recognize Croatia by Christmas 1991, no matter what the other members desired. In spite of all warning that such a move would lead to war, the Germans bullied the EC into recognizing Croatia and Slovenia. The breakup of Yugoslavia, a charter UN member and multi ethnic state, was thus assured. Americans had a right to know how and why such a disaster was created and what they were getting themselves into before sending 25,000 troops to enforce a peace that may or may not come about.

Americans have good reason to be less than enthusiastic in following the advice of those who push for some sort of "pax Americana." With all its irrationalities, the Cold War was based in good part on military, economic, and political issues. Its end raises questions in the minds of many Americans regarding why America must continue to intervene in the internal affairs of other countries. Policy makers have provided little in the way of an adequate reason other than the need for military and foreign policy bureaucracies to perpetuate themselves and reluctance to abandon the heady notion of American hegemony. It may well be time to focus on a host of domestic problems that make America an unpalatable role model for other nations.

NOTES

1. See, for instance, the early discussion of this trend by Gottfried Haberler, "Integration and Growth of the World Economy in Historical Perspective," *American Economic Review* (March 1964); pp. 1–22; George Macesich, *Integration and Stabilization: A Monetary View* (Westport, CT: Praeger, 1996).

2. Haberler, "Integration and Growth of the World Economy in Historical Perspective," p. 1.

3. Ibid., p. 2.

4. For review of issues, see, for instance, Felix Rohatyn, "World Capital: The Need and the Risks," *The New York Review of Books* (July 14, 1994); pp. 48–53.

5. Ibid., p. 48.

6. Ibid., p. 53.

7. See George Macesich, *Integration and Stabilization: A Monetary View*, p.13.

8. See George Macesich, *Transformation and Emerging Markets* (Westport, CT: Praeger, 1996).

Chapter 2

The United States Economy

A LOOK AHEAD

Most economic and political observers of the American scene will agree that achieving the country's full economic potential in the coming years should not be taken for granted. Rather, it will depend on how successful Americans are in promoting an open global market, encouraging savings and investment, and maintaining a healthy monetary and financial system. Most importantly, achieving sustainable economic growth in the future will depend on America's ability to foster and maintain price stability over time.

The United States is, in fact, the world's largest economy and single largest exporter. It has a vital interest in a continuing commitment to open international markets for goods and services. In a global economy that is increasingly interdependent, international trade is a vitally important factor in stimulating growth. Trade liberalization does have short-term costs in that some industries must adapt to increased competition. However, these costs tend to be outweighed in the long run by the benefits of growing export markets and lower prices for consumers. On balance, the American economy will derive long-run benefits from an expansion in world markets that stimulates exports and new job creation.

A crucial element in America's long-term growth is the provision of a positive climate for savings and investment. The United States must put in place effective incentives for business firms to make productive investment decisions. At the same time, the United States must encourage households and businesses to generate the savings necessary to finance investments. Some observers have noted on this score that the American economy has fallen short of other industrialized countries. For instance, the American personal savings rate in recent years has been little better than 4 percent of income. This rate appears to be about one half that of Japan and Germany. Private investment spending also appears to fall short of such investment in those two countries.

In good part, this American shortfall in investment can be attributed to larger federal government budget deficits, which have absorbed financial resources from the private sector. Some observers view the long-term outlook for reduction in the deficit as less than encouraging. Their concern turns, in particular, on entitlement programs and the long-term trends of such programs. In their view, controlling these expenditures will be difficult.

The importance of a stable monetary and financial system in promoting long-term prospects for the economy is underscored. On this score, the recent strengthening of American commercial banking will certainly enhance the flow of savings and investment to their most productive uses. Indeed, improved profitability and higher capitalization have allowed banks to put problem loans behind them and so be better equipped to meet the requirements of an expanding economy.

Given the rapid pace of globalization, there are important implications for America's monetary and financial organization. In particular, the growing interdependence of world financial markets increases the likelihood that economic or financial problems in one country may spread to other countries. The growing use of new types of financial instruments, such as derivatives, promises to complicate already difficult problems. A case in point are the experiences of financial institutions, corporations, and municipalities with derivatives. A number of these institutions experienced significant losses from these instruments. It is little wonder that in such a changing environment, among regulators in the Untied States and abroad, greater sophistication and understanding of the risks involved is required, as well as a greater degree of international cooperation among regulators.

Price stability will likely continue to play a critical role in future prosperity. An environment of stable prices contributes to higher potential economic growth by promoting productive investment and savings decisions. Indeed, based on experiences of the 1960s, 1970s, and 1980s, we have ample evidence of how quickly an increase in inflationary expectations can be built into market interest rates and so distort savings and investment decisions. Inflation is a monetary phenomenon. For this reason, among others, the role of monetary policy in promoting price stability is critical.

The many restructurings and downsizings in the American economy, especially since the early 1990s, is a cause of considerable anxiety for many Americans. These developments have taken place against the background of the economy's leading indicators between 1992 and 1995, which showed strength rarely seen since the 1950s. Investment has been growing swiftly, and productivity has been rising at twice the rate of the 1970s and 1980s. Productivity is a basic measure of economic efficiency, which to a large extent determines the living standards of most Americans. To many observers, productivity is the primary source of economic growth, and its increase is the answer to stagnant real wages.

The source of American anxiety over the economy is suggested by Census Bureau reports of the median family income in 1994, which was $38,782, adjusted for inflation. This figure is 1 percent below the level for 1991, and there was no increase in 1995. This recent stagnation, moreover, is part of a longer downward trend that has been taking place since the early 1970s. Indeed, 80 percent of working Americans whose jobs fall below the higher executive, managerial, and technical levels and under the heading "production and nonsupervisory workers" registered a drop in their weekly earnings adjusted for inflation by more than 18 percent between 1973 and 1995. By contrast, between 1979 and 1989 the real annual pay of corporate chief executives increased by 19 percent, and by 66 percent after taxes. For the bulk of American workers the renewed growth of productivity during the 1990s has not brought renewed growth in real wages. In fact, the economic recovery of the early 1990s for the first time in American post-World War II history failed to register an increase in the real wages of most American workers.

The growing inequality of income in the United States has raised the concern of many observers. According to some observers, this inequality could become a major threat to American society. It could produce a society that could turn harsh and cruel and be worried about future prospects. The continuing globalization of the world economy does impose a stringent discipline on its participants.[1] Felix Rohatyn, senior partner of the Wall Street investment bankers Lazard Fréres, described well the contemporary economic and social scene as a huge transfer of wealth from lower-skilled middle-class American workers to the owners of capital assets and to a new technological elite, whose compensation is tied to stock values.

IMPACT OF GLOBALIZATION

I have argued elsewhere that recent globalization of the world and American economies can, in good part, be attributed to the fall of communism and to the ability of business to organize production anywhere in the world with the objectives of minimizing costs and maximizing profits.[2] These developments have been aided and encouraged by ready access to information technologies. The result is a new mass-production economy at a worldwide level.

In manufacturing, for instance, there has been the advent of worldwide "lean production."[3] This is a technique pushed by the Japanese and now incorporated throughout the industrial world. It consists of three elements: Products must be easy to assemble (i.e., they must have manufacturability); workers must be less specialized in their skills; and stocks of inventory must be less costly to maintain, which is the so-called just-in-time method, whereby components arrive at the assembly plant with a minimal of expenditures in warehousing and financing.

Another important change has occurred in service industries such as banking and insurance, and communications where reengineering has transformed the workplace and led to a significant downsizing of the work force, especially in clerical and middle management positions. Many of these skills are now incorporated into software packages and placed into desktop computers.

Both reengineering and lean production have radically changed manufacturing industries such as automobiles and electronics, and service industries such as banking and insurance. Analysts have underscored the significant impact of these two innovations on employment. In particular, these innovations have reduced the amount of high-wage effort needed to produce a product and/or service of a given description. One of the key selling points for these innovations is their increased reliance on less-skilled and lower-paid workers. Of course, corporations achieving higher productivity gains while eliminating entire categories of skilled labor are unlikely to pass such savings on to their remaining and less-skilled workers. This helps to explain the failure of wages for many workers to benefit from rising productivity.

Other causes for the disparity between productivity and wages also come to mind readily. For instance, many firms can reduce costs even more by contracting out as much production as possible to smaller, independent producers whose wage costs may be even lower. Thus the practice is now well entrenched in such industries as automobile parts, machine tools, computers, and electronics. Again, Japanese firms have pushed the practice and now are followed by their competitors worldwide. As the production processes become simpler, a contract supplier can perform most tasks as efficiently as the principal firm. Many of the workers hired by contract suppliers, moreover, are not union members and so tend to be lower paid and receive fewer benefits.

It is people with the ability and skill to create and control the software and hardware that make reengineering a viable and profitable venture. They determine how contemporary and future firms will operate. The sophistication and sensitivity of the people carrying out the changes also determine the success of reengineering.

In particular, it is becoming increasingly clear that lean production and reengineering have had a singular and diverse impact on people who work for wages and salaries and those who own capital and benefit from interest and dividends. Analysts report that employees' share of increased revenue fell dramatically during the past ten years. One observer compares the distribution of income gains in 1993 to the pattern prevailing between 1981 and 1989; the share going to wage earners fell from 52 percent to 38 percent; the share paid out as capital income remained constant at 28 percent.[4] The share going to wage earners was the lowest in recent memory. It may well be that the American dream exceeds the grasp of too many Americans, as some observers have noted. In their view, the central problem of the 1990s has been more the maldistribution of wealth than the failure to increase overall wealth.

During the recovery of the 1990s, growth has been strong enough to push stock prices, corporate profits, and the pay of CEOs to record levels, while the pay and living standards of many Americans have continued to stagnate. Little wonder that people look to ways to curb excessive concentration of power in the hands of corporate interests. These concerns have led Senator Bill Bradley to propose that employers should be obliged by law not only to cover the medical insurance of long-serving former employees, but also to contribute substantially to an employee's retraining costs. Employee pensions, argues Bradley, should be fully transferrable from one job to another. Certainly, these measures would help victims of reengineering and downsizing.

IN SEARCH OF SOLUTIONS

Other observers suggest European-style works councils as a way to give white-collar employees as well as blue-collar workers extensive rights of co-determination. Illustrations of co-determination are provided by the German and Dutch models, in which management must obtain the agreement of the employees' council on such matters as reengineering and training. Co-determination also tends to be incorporated in employee-owned businesses.

Essentially, many of the solutions suggested by various people involve some sort of reordering of priorities to put more emphasis on protecting employees. This can mean concessions by both workers and management to make sure an enterprise or firm remains strong enough to preserve jobs. It can mean a willingness by industry and even taxpayers to spend more to help workers through the transition from one job to another. It can mean drawing on the experience of other countries that lay off workers only as a last resort. And, of course, it can also mean making workers more self-reliant in dealing with their current and future employment and careers.

Markets and technologies change rapidly. Many a former industry blue-chip firm found itself unable to meet market competition from leaner, smaller, and more price- and quality-conscious firms. To meet these changes, some firms have downsized in a violent and overly hasty reaction to changing times. They shed workers without changing their strategies or the way they work. Many of these firms, if they survive, end up with a demoralized work force and no new business. In too many instances, downsizing is simply viewed as a financial exercise.

It is now generally agreed that deep cuts can cripple product development, marketing, and customer service. As business vanishes, management is forced to undertake still more cuts. In rare instances management may even admit its mistakes and hire again.

Employee ownership may not always live up to its ideal. Employee ownership experiments such as at Weirton Steel and Wire have dissolved in bitter recriminations. Another recent experiment is United Airlines. There are now periodic rumblings of dissatisfaction at United. United's new employees work for lower starting pay and a somewhat smaller stake in United than those who were around before the employee buyout, creating two classes of workers. Moreover, United employees who elected to take no pay cuts and thus got no stake in the company often complain that the employee-owners treat them just as the old manager did. Nothing, moreover, will insulate even the employee-owned firm from the competitive realities of markets and technologies in the long run.

Many people turn to education and training as the best defense for workers in an uncertain economy. Some firms make a serious effort to provide resources for the continuing training and education of their employees. Intel Corporation, a maker of the microchip used in personal computers, spends more than $120 million on training, or nearly $3,000 averaged across all of its workers, more than double the national average.[5]

As for self-reliance, many downsized employees find it the only viable alternative to dealing with their futures. The lesson is simple enough. Government and businesses can do some things, but in the final analysis workers have little to fall back on but themselves.

POLITICAL REACTION

Not surprisingly, globalization and its impact has prompted political reaction. Throughout American history, political movements have responded to challenges of globalization with varying degrees of success. Indeed, the American political party system in good measure turned on what kind of economy and protection was desirable. The contest between Alexander Hamilton and Thomas Jefferson in the early years of the United States is a case in point. Jefferson's agrarian vision that Americans should be sturdily independent rural yeomen collided with Hamilton's vision, which favored a restless, urban, and entrepreneurial society.

The argument continued into President Andrew Jackson's war against the Second Bank of the United States in the 1830s, into the pre–Civil War debate about free labor versus wage labor, and into later debates about laissez faire versus unionization and free trade versus protectionism. Little wonder that in the 1996 political campaigns for president, various candidates promised to assuage American anxiety and protect job security, rekindling the old debate about how much economic dynamism is desirable and the costs of such dynamism with regard to the tranquility of individuals, the stability of communities, and America's character.

Thus it is that on more than one occasion in their history, Americans have rediscovered populism and its power. The old language of populism seeks to stir up antiestablishment fervor. Throughout American history, populist voices have spoken to both the fears and the hopes of ordinary people.

It is understandable, of course, that many observers wish to distance themselves from the darker side of populism. Unfortunately, populism is as promising and as troublesome as democracy itself. It is easy to accuse a relatively small privileged elite of taking wealth and power from the people. The exercise tends to stimulate public debate and may even hasten needed changes. Unfortunately, it also invites conspiracy thinking.

Consider President Andrew Jackson, who did much to create American populism's dual nature. He rallied small farmers and craftsmen in the 1820s and 1830s to take part in the political activities of the country. At the same time, he was also an accomplished ethnic cleanser who threw the Cherokee Indians off their ancestral lands. He did not repudiate slavery.

Jackson's penchant for demonizing his rivals is well known. He vetoed the renewal of the charter of the Second Bank of the United States, arguing that the Bank was a monopoly controlled by wealthy Easterners. To this he added that more than a quarter of the Bank's stock was owned by foreigners. All the while, of course, Jackson understood perfectly well that a growing economy needed banks and bankers. Witness, for instance, his withdrawal of federal government deposits from the Second Bank and their transfer to state banks. Nevertheless, his rhetoric portrayed bankers as parasites and worse who used the money of industrious people to make a fortune for themselves.

Again in the 1890s, a third political party, the People's Party, gave populism its name. It promoted both grass-roots democracy and the inflated notion that plutocrats were gleefully impoverishing average Americans. The People's Party wanted to transform a system in which railroads charged farmers as much as they could bear and the federal courts helped employers break up unions and avoid regulation. The Party advocated a total ban on alien ownership of land and looked with disdain on the big Eastern cities in America. Many of the Party's "true believers" came overwhelmingly from the rural and Protestant South and West.

The Great Depression in the 1930s inspired an energetic renewal of rhetorical assaults on the monied and the privileged, although this sentiment was always present in American society. In the subsequent upheaval of the 1930s, most people tried to alleviate the pain of the jobless and hungry. Indeed, the United States owes such reforms as the Social Security system to the populist push for reform. The demagogy of such people as Father Charles Coughlin, who told his 1930s radio audience that the Rothschilds and other international bankers had planned the Great Depression to create an artificial scarcity of money, had an influence on society. For his part, Louisiana's Huey Long promised to make "every man a king and every woman a queen" by means of taxing the savings of the rich. Not to be outdone, organizations such as the Congress of Industrial Organization and particularly its militant wing accused antiunion industrialists, including Henry Ford, of being quasi-fascists.

In the postwar period, much of the populist rhetoric was updated. It exposed big government as a conspiracy against the average American. From Senator Joseph McCarthy's charge that the elite was selling out America, to House Speaker Newt Gingrich's claim that a liberal elite is the enemy of the average American, the political extremists made the welfare state appear to be the antithesis of every self-reliant American. In the mid-1990s, Pat Buchanan underscored that big money can indeed wreck the lives of working Americans at least as painfully as federal bureaucrats can regulate them. This idea of Wall Street versus Main Street misses the point that many Americans now own stock directly or through their pension funds. In fact, the very protectionism urged by newly minted populists could make matters even worse for all Americans.

There is legitimate concern with easing the transition costs for the displaced or downsized worker. It is obvious that the most highly trained and educated workers at all levels fare best in an economy undergoing adjustment. Unfortunately, the government alone cannot invest anything close to the estimated $1 trillion to $3 trillion needed to improve the training and education of those hardest hit. For its part, the private sector suggests that many firms have cut their training budgets. Moreover, higher education is increasingly beyond the reach of low-income Americans. From 1980 to 1994, average tuition rose 70 percent after inflation at public two-year colleges and 86 percent at four-year institutions.

Most discussions about how to change America's education system to make it more responsive to the modern economy get bogged down in arguments over who should be setting the rules. Thus the federal government has opposed even experimental efforts to provide vouchers to families that want help paying for education outside the public schools for fear that doing so could undercut public education. Some firms have gone so far as to locate only in towns where states and local school districts institute high standards; presumably the rest of the country would then pour resources into education in the hopes of attracting investment. However, most executives say education is the province of the government, not the private sector. Matters are not made easier by the obvious fact that most government-led worker retraining programs have been hopelessly out of touch with the needs of the economy.

There is skepticism about the ability or will of government to find a solution to the education and employment problems facing the economy. It may well be, as some observers argue, that the big initiatives are going to have to start in the business world. Indeed, failure to face up to the problem may bring a political backlash analogous to the political upheaval of the 1890s, which forced the "robber barons" to break up their powerful trust and submit to regulation. It was impossible to foresee that from the chaos of the 1890s the extensive regulation of business would spring quickly.

NOTES

1. George Macesich, *Transformation and Emerging Markets* (Westport, CT: Praeger, 1996).

2. Ibid.

3. See Simon Head, "The New, Restless Economy," *The New York Review,* February 29, 1996, pp. 47–52.

4. Ibid., p. 50.

5. David E. Sanger and Steve Lohr, "A Search for Answers to Avoid the Layoffs," *The New York Times*, Saturday, March 9, 1996, p. 10.

Chapter 3

Global or Transnational Enterprise

TRANSNATIONAL ENTERPRISE

It is very difficult to know how many companies in America are foreign owned and how many American companies are located in other countries. We do know that totally globalized American firms are rare. In fact, most multinational firms tend to be more national or even regional than global in everything from membership of their boards to the distribution of their shareholdings to the composition of their suppliers. Apparently, there are limits to the globalization of firms. Nevertheless, firms do produce goods and services where they find best the combination of price and quality and distribute them wherever they can discover or create a demand.

It is useful to consider the global or transnational corporation, firm, or enterprise in perspective. A corporation becomes transnational or multinational when its management begins to plan, organize, and control its international production on a worldwide scale. National markets, in effect, become segments of broader regional and world markets. For our purposes, a transnational corporation is defined as an enterprise that takes part in foreign production through its own affiliates, exercises direct control over the policies of its affiliates, and seeks to follow a worldwide strategy.

In the continuing discussions of transnational corporations or multinational enterprises, there tends to be agreement that (1) transnational corporations make a significant contribution to total welfare; (2) not all parties share the benefits equally or at all (this appears to be the case not only between the host country and home country but indeed between labor and capital); and (3) political, economic, and social considerations all point to the need for companies to adopt policies that are less dominated by the interests of the home country's organizations. The challenge, of course, is to develop policies that effectively deal with these issues while at the same time allowing the transnational corporation to make its contribution to worldwide welfare. In host countries that differ in one or another aspect depending in part on whether they are developed or developing, a transnational corporation affects the elite, often challenges ideologies, and results in a clash of cultures. In the home countries the transnational corporation often adds to a feeling that control is lost, jurisdictional conflicts increase, and psychic pain at times tends to conceal any benefits derived, especially where sensitive defense issues may be concerned.

For instance, as a rule, in the formulation and execution of science policy, governments channel growth and subsidies to indigenously owned enterprises. This is understandable since governments as a rule have not been anxious to subsidize the research of U.S.-owned subsidiaries. Similar policies, for instance, are followed in Canada, Great Britain, and France. Indeed, the disposition of public agencies to favor locally owned producers is being formalized and strengthened in many countries.

SOME MISCONCEPTIONS

The importance of transnational corporations is but another manifestation of the globalization of the world's economy. These corporations represent an important element in promoting trade and development worldwide. As such, they serve to integrate the international economy and provide many small, emerging countries access to world markets.

In discussing transnational corporations, it is useful to dispel at the outset several misconceptions regarding their role and stance, especially in emerging market countries. First, emerging countries are not as important to the transnational corporations as is often argued. Except in the case of extractive mining and the oil industry, the bulk of transnatinal corporations' sales, revenues, profits, and growth are earned in industrial countries. This is particularly true for the world's major manufacturing, distributive, and financial corporations.

Second, more than resources from abroad are needed to trigger and sustain economic growth and development in a country. Domestic resources must be energized to have a multiplier effect. Moveover, the ability of a country to absorb resources profitably and effectively may be limited due to domestic factors.

Third, the transnational corporation, by effectively and efficiently integrating and allocating resources on a worldwide scale, does so not at the expense of the host country but assists in integrating its host country into the international economy. At the same time, the transnational corporation may provide the host country with bargaining leverage that it otherwise would not have. A policy of self-sufficiency is not possible for even the best-endowed country. Integration of the productive capacities and advantages of developing countries into the international economy is the most sensible approach.

Further, the parent corporation seldom, if ever, has 100 percent ownership of a transnational enterprise. There is agreement that 100 percent ownership may be desirable since it is likely to make unity-of-action planning and other related activities easier (hence the idea of restricting a foreigner to a minority participation). On the other hand, the increasing scarcity of capital may push transnational enterprises to insist on host country participation in various forms, such as joint venture with local capital and partnerships. The host country may be increasingly reluctant to enter such arrangements, viewing them as drains on already scarce local capital. For all its difficulties, mixed ownership of transnational enterprises may become increasingly favored, especially if world scarcity of capital continues.

THE ECONOMICS OF TRANSNATIONAL ENTERPRISE

The objectives of a firm are not always clear cut. This is true for the transnational enterprise as it is for others. Simply asking a firm's managers what their objectives are does not necessarily yield satisfactory results. One soon discovers that managers agree to any plausible objective about which they are asked. Transnational enterprise managers say they wish to maximize their own incomes (pecuniary and nonpecuniary), maximize the firm's profits, maximize the firm's sales, minimize costs, minimize government (domestic and host) intervention, and at the same time increase and develop overseas affiliates. Since it is seldom possible to serve simultaneously a multiplicity of such goals, it is more important to determine what these managers do rather than what they say they do. Even the most casual observer will discover that they settle on one objective or some compromise among them.

This is simply another way of saying that a transnational enterprise will seek to maximize pecuniary and nonpecuniary profits. An enterprise's decision thus can be analyzed without recourse to a kind of budget restraint, whose existence distinguishes the traditional analysis of the firm from that of consumers. In fact, extending theories of the firm are able to explain much of the behavior of transnational enterprises.

The problem that some analysts consider important is that of a transnational corporation composed of a large number of geographically diverse operating units.[1] Thus the corporation may pursue profit maximization while one affiliate seems to accept some inefficiency (for instance, encouraging a young management group); another affiliate attempts to maximize roles at a very low profit goal to ensure market share in a market with long-run growth; and a third affiliate in an emerging country location is given considerable managerial leeway for political reasons to ensure access to raw materials and minimize risks of confiscation.

The economics of the transnational enterprise tend to be approached from the viewpoint of oligopoly theory. This theoretical situation is characterized by mutual interdependence among various sellers as a result of a small number of sellers in a particular market area. It is also one of the most complex portions of price theory since oligopoly is not a single clear-cut case. It includes a wide range of related cases all characterized by mutual interdependence but differing in the exact degree of interdependency and the exact policies followed by firms.

Oligopoly, in the sense of mutual interdependence, arises whenever the number of firms is sufficiently small that a price change by any one firm affects the sales of the other firms to such an extent that readjustments are made by these firms. If there are only two or three or eight or nine producers of a product in an industry, oligopoly will obviously exist. Given the complexities and diversities of oligopoly, the analysis is usually broken down into several segments.

Consider, first, complete oligopoly, in which relationships among firms are sufficiently close to permit maximization of the joint profits of the firms as a group. Such a situation may occur as a result of spontaneous coordination of policies among several firms or conscious cooperation of the firms' managers.

Maximization of joint profits requires determination of the total demand schedule for the product and summation of the marginal cost curves of the several firms. By collective action in the case of collusion, firms will estimate the demand and cost schedules and set the optimum price and output. If prices are set by one firm and followed by all others, this firm will attempt to price on the basis of the total demand and cost schedules rather than on its own and other firms will go along with the decision of this firm. In the absence of collusion, maximum joint profits can be obtained only if each firm, acting independently, correctly estimates the price that is the optimum from the standpoint of the group on the basis of the firm's estimate of the total demand schedule for the product.

Total profits are shared by the various firms according to relative costs and sales. The firms with the lowest costs and those with large sales volumes will obtain the largest amounts. But this, in turn, depends on relative consumer preference for the several brands. In the case of collusion among firms, agreed-upon market shares and profit division will likely depend on the relative bargaining strength of the firms. Such strength, in turn, is likely to depend on bargaining skill, ability to carry out threats successfully, relative costs, and consumer preference.

Attainment of complete oligopoly is a difficult task. Firms simply do not surrender their freedom of action easily, especially if they are under pressure to increase their share of the total market and thus to increase their profit. It is most unlikely that demand and cost schedules for all firms will be identical or required by the maximum joint-profit price. Such a situation would require closings of high-cost firms and concentration of production in lower-cost firms. The issue, of course, is to select firms that are to close. The result likely will be to compromise on price. Such a compromise will not be readily accepted by all firms, so there is an incentive to break away from competitive pricing.

Moreover, the problems of estimating the total demand curve will make selection of the optimum price difficult since various firms likely will have different views about the optimum. The net result will be that actual selection will depend on the bargaining power of the several firms. In addition, optimum profit maximization may depend on other objectives. For example, some objectives may include forcing other firms to carry out desired policies, or to drive other firms out of business, or to test bargaining power.

Difficulties in reaching an agreement are also compounded by other factors influencing the attainment of maximum group profits, such as the failure of firms to agree on product changes, advertising policies, and introduction of new technologies. Each firm is reluctant to come to an agreement when it feels confident that it can do better in any or all of these areas than the others. Price changes lead to changes by competitors that a given firm may not be able to meet. As a result, there is a tendency to reach price agreements more readily. The fact is, however, that profits will eventually be eroded for the oligopoly group through price competition.

Even if agreement among existing firms in an oligopoly group regarding maximum-profit price is forthcoming, there is usually fear that such a price may encourage new firms to enter. The existence of excessive profits serves as an incentive to new firms, which may overcome barriers to entry such as large capital requirements, established reputations and relationships, and large volume output. The net result is that firms may deliberately hold prices below the optimum short-run, maximum-profit levels. They may prefer so-called lower reasonable profits rather than risk and encourage the entrance of new firms.

In addition, difficulties in coordinating the action of several firms in an oligopoly reduce the likelihood of frequent price changes even in the face of changing circumstances. Conditions and circumstances do change so that even if the price set originally is one yielding maximum joint profit, it is unlikely to do so for any length of time.

The net effect is that difficulties in establishing a maximum joint profit for an oligopoly group render such an exercise largely futile, even under the best of cooperative circumstances among firms. The fact is that little mutual interdependence exists among firms, especially as the number increases to bring about a mutually satisfactory price yield and optimum joint profit. These difficulties lead economists to turn to partial oligopoly theory.

Partial oligopoly theory deals with situations in which joint profits of the group are not maximized. Such cases may be spontaneous coordination on a limited scale rather than agreement among firms. The essential difference between the price setting by oligopolists and that by other firms is the importance of the influence on the firms' demand schedules of possible reactions by competitors. In effect, interdependence will likely lead to reduced elasticity of the demand schedule of the product of the firm beneath what it would be in the absence of such interdependence.

There is also the tendency to create considerable uncertainty regarding the exact nature of demand schedules facing firms since a firm can seldom be certain about the exact reaction of other firms to a price increase or decrease. A price reduction by one firm may lead to a significant change, an insignificant change, or no change at all in its sales volume accordingly as competitors take appropriate action. For all practical purposes, the firm may be faced with several demand schedules depending on the reaction of other firms. Firms then have an incentive to minimize the frequency of price changes and/or resort to techniques of pricing that minimize reaction on the part of other firms.

One means for reducing the degree of uncertainty is simply not to make independent price changes but rather to adopt and follow policies and prices set by other firms. This is the price leader situation that is so typical, some argue, in oligopoly. Thus a leading firm producing a large portion of total output tends to dominate the pricing. Smaller firms are then presumably able to sell as much as they wish at the price established by the leading firm. This is achieved by the larger firm setting price through pricing techniques. Although these techniques are not likely to minimize profits for the firms as a group, they may represent the best possible solution. This is consistent with the assumption that firms seek to maximize profits. The essence is that the use of average-cost pricing or cost-plus pricing provides a relatively simple method of price setting and adjustment that minimizes competitive disturbances, particularly if more or less uniform methods of allocation of common costs to various products are followed.

Under oligopoly conditions, considerable opportunity is provided for the use of product variation, advertising, and other forms of selling activities. Since price tends to stabilize at a given figure and price reductions are dangerous, in order to expand sales and thus lower average cost, firms typically turn to other safer forms of selling activities as a means of increasing their sales. Competition can readily meet price cuts, but nonprice competition is more subtle and so more difficult to match.

Nonetheless, within oligopoly there appears to be a feeling of interdependence with respect to selling activities, just as there is with respect to prices. In the case of perfect collusion, for instance, firms may agree and select product and selling policies so that profits for the group are maximized. Again, perfect collusion is seldom if ever achieved. Indeed, the scattered evidence that exists suggests that firms are even less likely to agree on a common course of selling and product policies than on a price policy. For reasons discussed previously, firms feel on steadier ground in following independent policies regarding selling and product than they do in following price changes, whereas competitors are likely to follow suit quietly.

The absence of complete collusion among firms drives them into increasing their activities to increase their share of the market. Competitors, of course, will follow suit. The net effect likely will be to cancel out much of the selling activity efforts, and some of the firms will gain in sales volume. If firms are aware of interdependence in such activities, they are less likely to engage in them.

As in other imperfect market situations, such as monopoly, price discrimination may be practiced in oligopoly. It will, however, require more imagination to carry out since firms must agree on the prices to be charged in different markets or independently follow identical price policies. Such cooperation is unlikely, so price discrimination is less likely than under complete monopoly.

Thus far our concern with oligopoly theory has been of the short-run variety. The long-run variety allows industry to grow or to decline, resources to move from one industry to another, and investors and persons entering the labor force to choose among industries. In many of the big oligopolistic industries, in the long run, technological change occurs and consumer demands shift. New products for consumers come on the market as new machines, new processes, and new materials appear in the production function of firms. In the long run, demands are more elastic.

The net effect is that over the long run, there is a tendency toward uniform levels of profits in the oligopolistic industries, as in others, to prevail given the mobility of resources over time. The tendency is proximate since some barriers to entry persist. The point is that monopolistic elements in oligopoly seem to become less important in the long run. There is a tendency that the allocation of resources under oligopoly is, by and large, tolerably close to efficiency. There are pressures to reduce costs, and production does appear responsive to consumer demand.

Oligopoly, then, is a form of competition. As a representation of reality, this model is certainly not an impossibility. Noncollusive behavior of this kind, based on good if not perfect information, must sometimes occur. We shall consider the empirical importance as it applies to transnational enterprise. But let us consider first a cartel model, which is usually looked on as merely a temporary form of oligopoly.

A cartel is an explicit agreement, typically informal, among independent firms (or countries) on prices, output, and usually on matters such as division of geographical sales. Treating of cartels under the heading of oligopoly is accepted by most economists for several reasons. Cartels are usually shortterm. Firms do have the desire for large joint projects and so the desire to form cartels. Firms are likely, however, to disagree over the division of joint profits. This tendency is a leading factor in the breakup of cartel arrangements.

Analysis of cartel situations is usefully divided into perfect cartels and imperfect cartels. A perfect cartel is an agreement among firms in an industry that results in maximization of joint profits of the member firms. The coordinating organization presumably has full knowledge of the demand for the output of the industry at each possible price. As a result, the coordinating organization can calculate marginal revenue for the industry. It also knows the marginal cost of all the firms and can calculate the marginal cost of each volume of output for the industry. The organization then sets marginal revenue equal to marginal cost. This gives the price and output at which the firm's marginal cost equals the level of industry marginal cost selected to maximize joint profits of the industry.

Imperfect cartels originate in the fact that firms are unwilling to give up all their sovereignty, as would be required under a perfect cartel. They wish to retain their identity and freedom of action. This means that although imperfect cartels can raise prices and profits, they do not reach the levels of monopoly.

In general, after fixing price a cartel usually must set sales or output quotas. This does not have to be done if industry demand is growing as fast as or faster than the expansion of industry output. Typically, however, output quotas have to be set to maintain the cartel price. The method whereby the division of profits is to take place usually leads to conflict. There is an incentive to cut price secretly and chisel in every way and means possible since additional sales at covertly negotiated lower prices are profitable.

These are, in essence, the more important oligopoly theories. It is important to note that there are several hypotheses regarding price and output under oligopoly. The result is that economic theory cannot give much support to economic policy. More useful models of oligopoly would assist considerably in improving the standards of economic regulation. These issues are already highly complex on the domestic scene, and the U.S. government attempts to regulate radio and television broadcasting in metropolitan market areas, air transportation, and the like. Attempts to do so on the international level are even more complex.

Application of oligopoly theories to problems of economic policy, however, is difficult. Lack of a set of agreed-on models of oligopoly means that economic theory cannot give much support to economic policy. We can only hope that the future will bring advances in oligopoly theory that will lead to economic policy directed toward dealing with these issues and applying them in formulating economic policy.

In fact, the models of oligopoly discussed draw prices and outputs ranging between monopoly and perfect competition. For oligopoly to have the same price and output as monopoly, the necessary assumptions are uniformity of costs and products, perfect knowledge, no objective other than profit maximization, and either the mutual recognition of uniformity and interdependence or the actions of the perfect cartel. Price leadership, imperfect cartel, and incomplete collusion can give results close to monopoly or perfect competition. They can give prices and output between the extraneous. As a result, theory cannot say much that helps in assessing the performance of oligopolistic industries.

As for nonprice competition, there is consensus that quality and advertising can be competitive variables. How nonprice competition affects economic welfare is difficult to say at this point in the development of oligopoly theory.

In summary, the interdependence of firms in oligopoly markets, where a firm's action and the reaction of other firms result in shifting revenue and cost curves for all firms in the market, appears to lead to indeterminate outcomes. By making special restrictive assumptions, oligopoly theorists have been able to build models that yield determinate results, but this has led to nearly as many theories of oligopoly as there are oligopoly theorists. Oligopoly markets are considered by many analogous to a poker game, wherein elements of strategy and bluff play important roles. For this reason, some theorists have attempted to apply the theory of games to the analysis of oligopoly markets, but as yet there have been no satisfactory results.

Concern with oligopoly theory and other monopolistic tendencies raises major questions of public policy toward firms with monopoly power. This concern is typically expressed with transnational enterprises as well, since many people view them as containing elements of monopoly power. Do product differentiation and advertising waste resources, or do they result in greater welfare in terms of the variety of goods in the market? Are oligopoly firms an undesirable locus of economic and political power resulting in misallocation of resources, or is their size necessary to capture all the economies of scale available in a modern technical society? If oligopolies are undesirable, should these firms be reduced in size by international and national antitrust action, or should the size of the firms be left alone and the firms either controlled or owned by the host government? The fact is that economic analysis may not answer these questions to the satisfaction of everyone concerned.

EMPIRICAL EVIDENCE

The existing empirical evidence have is consistent with the profit-maximizing behavior of transnational corporations. So, too, is evidence suggesting that oligopoly models do provide useful insights into the operations of transnational corporations. Admittedly, these are bits and pieces of evidence gathered from various sources and by various means including interview evidence, which is open to various interpretations. Thus growth and profits are often synonymous with profit-maximizing behavior as reported by interview studies. Other analysts suggest that on occasion transnational corporate behavior is not simply disguised profit maximization.

Expenditures on foreign plants and equipment and the flow of direct investment tend to be attributed to profit-maximizing behavior. Oligopolistic interdependence is also suggested in the "bunching" of entry consistent with U.S. industry concentration indexes and with the profitability of investment abroad in the relevant industry. In essence, transnational enterprise behavior can be viewed as a form of constrained profit maximization, in which financial, structural, environmental, and general resource variables limit the pursuit of maximum profits.

On the issue of whether large oligopolistic industries are leaders in introducing innovation and change, scattered evidence suggests that there are relatively few research-intensive corporations that are not at the same time transnational. On the sensitive issue of centralization and decentralization of distribution of innovative research and development (R&D) as between parent and affiliate, a good case can be made for either view. Concentrating R&D in the home country reduces problems associated with financial control, costs of communication and policing, and potential divergence from central product policies. Cultural problems and differences of coordinating R&D may also be reduced by centralization.

If we look at only R&D expenditure by large transnational enterprises, the innovation picture may be distorted. For instance, evidence suggests that large firms may be more important in minor improvement inventions and that small firms and independent inventors are the principal source of basic inventions and major breakthroughs. Indeed, these issues merge into the strategies of oligopoly. Each may seek to let the others bear the brunt of risk, experiment, and high initial cost while waiting for the appropriate moment to step in and scoop up the major gains. When each waits for the other to take the first dangerous step, it is perfectly possible that that first step will not be taken at all.

Pricing practices of transnational enterprises theoretically can be sorted out with help from oligopoly theory. Empirical evidence to support such behavior is scarce. The scattered evidence that we have suggests that the cost-plus prices and negotiated prices familiar to oligopoly theory are in use with respect to transfer pricing in intrafirm transactions between parent and subsidiaries. These practices may also apply to independent buyers. It is difficult to say how widespread the practice of manipulative transfer pricing is since managers are reluctant to admit to these practices, which are viewed as outside of market transactions and enable transnational enterprises to evade many of the checks on corporate behavior provided by national laws.

Some idea of the complexity of intrafirm transactions is suggested by its various forms, including (1) locating profits in an affiliate where the host country taxes are lower (and conversely restricting profits where taxes are higher); (2) withdrawing funds from an affiliate by increasing prices or goals sold to that affiliate by other affiliates or by the parent entity in a transnational enterprise network; and (3) financing an affiliate by reducing prices on goods sold to it by other affiliates or the parent organization. Still other forms are employed, such as juggling the allocation of overhead and joint costs, including R&D and advertising, and overpricing the plant and equipment used to set up or expand a foreign facility.

A transnational enterprise's decision to employ transfer pricing is encouraged by tariff barriers in effect in the importing country, the absolute and relative differences in tax rates among various countries, and a host government's policies regarding the remittance of profits, difficult labor relations, and currency restrictions. Strictly domestic incentives to employ transfer pricing include varying degrees of ownership of affiliates, and a desire to place profits where a firm enjoys the largest ownership position, and using techniques to allocate markets among affiliates.

Many a multinational enterprise ended the 1980s in worse shape than at the beginning of the decade. Such leading multinationals as Boeing, Caterpillar, Dayton-Hudson, DuPont, Salomon Brothers, Texas Instruments, and Xerox managed to run up huge losses.[2] Indeed, in 1991 Citicorp registered a loss of $457 million; General Motors, which more or less invented modern corporate management, saw a $23.5 billion loss in 1992; and in 1993 IBM, which had dominated every national market it entered, saw an $8.1 billion loss. In fact, the problems were not confined to American multinationals. Philips, a Dutch electronics giant, got into deep trouble, as did Germany's Daimler-Benz and Japan's Matsushita.

Globalization of the world economy has exposed the mutinationals' weaknesses. Deregulation and lower trade barriers have reduced the value of their carefully cultivated relationships with various country bureaucracies. The spread and sophistication of modern managerial techniques has undermined the monopoly of multinational managerial wisdom. Due to pirating of reverse engineering and other forms of industrial theft , multinationals no longer enjoy a monopoly of their own ideas. The spread of computerization and decline in the price of information now permits smaller firms to engage in the sort of information processing that was once the preserve of the large multinational firms.

The changes in many multinational firms in the 1990s have been dramatic. Many have changed their ideas about where their competitive advantage lies: It is no longer in capital resources per se, but in knowledge. They now view the chief task of management as ensuring that their knowledge is generated widely and used as efficiently as possible. In the process of doing so, many multinational enterprises have unloaded their excess baggage and are now much leaner and fitter than they have been for decades. As a result, they remain serious players in the global economy.

NOTES

1. See, for example, N. Hood and S. Young, *The Economics of the Multi-National Enterprise* (New York: Longman, 1979).

2. For example, see the survey of multinationals reported in *The Economist*, June 24, 1995, pp. 3–22.

Chapter 4

The Role of Government in the United States

THE ISSUE

The continuing U.S. effort to further globalize the world economy further and shrink the size and role of government is applauded and celebrated by Democrats and Republicans as well as mainstream parties of Europe and elsewhere. This is a formidable task given the penchant for government intervention by politicians, bureaucrats and others. In fact, the increased role of government in the public sector has been one of the singularly important modifications in the U.S. market-type economy. This chapter considers the growth of government intervention.

Observers underscore the growth in public education, the regulatory role of business imposed by government, and the importance of taxes and transfer payments in the transfer and redistribution of income. To these important roles of American government can be added various regulatory measures adopted to activate various social goals, including protection of the environment. The importance of the Social Security system has increased, as have various entitlement programs in the federal budget. The purchase of goods and services by government is a significant component in the United States' total aggregate demand. In addition, the U.S. government is the single largest employer in the U.S. economy.

FORCES PROMOTING INTERVENTION

Our discussion suggests the extent to which the American economy has been redefined by government intervention. Certainly, America's experience has encouraged such intervention. Experience with the Industrial Revolution and its upheaval and later events had much to do with the creation of interventionist ideas from theory to practice.

One consequence of the practice of interventionist ideas was increased authority of the state and its bureaucratic apparatus. This expansion was expedient but inglorious, necessary but dangerous, useful but costly. Along with the expansion came growing concern over the ability of the public to deal on equal terms with the maximizing behavior of an "artful and ever active" bureaucracy and political elite. Experience confirms that constraints must be placed on the exercise of discretionary authority by vote-maximizing bureaucrats and political elites if democracy is to thrive and prosper.[1]

The public must insist that such constraints be put in place. Indeed, it was that shrewd observer of American democracy, Alexis de Tocqueville, who warned in the first half of the nineteenth century that democracy could falter as a consequence of citizens' diminished interest in restraining central authority.[2]

Even earlier, the American founders—for instance, James Madison—were aware that their project, the federal constitution, was an exercise in constructing government out of defective human parts. They believed that the urge to tyrannize others was so strong that external restraints became absolutely indispensable. The image of man in their discourse appears less than free and rational because his will and intelligence may be at the service of his "passions," forces beyond himself that make self-control improbable. In both the Federalist and anti-Federalist political factions, a vague egalitarianism also led to the fear of elitism—"the artful and ever active aristocracy" usurping the power that belonged to an unalert and passive people, as Walter Lippmann succinctly put it when he informed Americans that the framers of the Constitution had bequeathed to future generations of Americans a government of checks and balances.

The task of constraining the bureaucracy and political elite is made all the more difficult by utopian attempts to make the uncertain certain by control of society according to plan. As I discuss elsewhere, monetary policy is but a case in point. Monetary uncertainty originating primarily from fluctuations in the purchasing power of money will tend to move the social order away from the use of money and markets toward a greater reliance on some form of greater government control or command organization, thereby strengthening bureaucracy and its political influence. Moreover, monetary instability and market failure are closely linked and both serve to weaken the social fabric.

Another illustration that will serve bureaucracy is the rise of socialism in the 1930s, which promoted central economic planning and the redistribution of income policies. The Keynesian Revolution stressed the failure of the economic system, which was avoidable by the application of scientific knowledge. Harry Johnson is surely correct when he writes that these two movements reinforced one another.[3] In turn, this led to the view that economic backwardness can be traced to the defects in the private enterprise system and market democracy, not to the backwardness of people and their cultures in relation to the requirements of modern industrial society. Indeed, in the 1960s many people in the Third World promoted this view to the top of the world's development agenda.[4]

THE STATE AND BUREAUCRACY

Rapid sociopolitical and economic change, particularly since the Great Depression, has brought with it a growing bureaucratic influence as well as increased demands for reform to constrain bureaucracy's taste for discretionary authority. This urgency is underscored by growing evidence from the experience of former socialist countries of Eastern Europe. The violations of public trust and confidence by domestic bureaucracies in those countries are now common knowledge.

The fact is, however, that a government and its bureaucracy do not operate in a vacuum. They are products of previous and present values and beliefs about what government should do and how it should be done. Modern bureaucracy is the result of cumulative theory and practice. Unlike the case of the former socialist, institutional change in general tends to be cumulative. Much of what we have and do today reflects lingering influences from the past. This is as true of countries undergoing the processes of reform as it is of more stable countries. The result is that the processes of reform are even more difficult and complex. Reformers must take into account that old ideas and vested interests never die but withdraw into enclaves, small and large, where their partisans prepare for and await the moment of return. Many interventionist ideas, as we have discussed, promoted more active government involvement and responsibility for the (1) conditions of the economy, (2) level of unemployment, (3) stability of prices, (4) advance of productivity, (5) rate of growth, (6) inequity and injustices in the distribution of revenue, (7) conditions of the environment, and (8) quality of life. These are expectations and responsibilities that only a very powerful government and its bureaucracy could meet. Government and its bureaucracy grew and expanded to meet these challenges. Such an expansion is certainly more than the liberal state envisioned. This is in contrast to a world of private societies, in which individuals are free to engage and disengage in trade or any other form of social intercourse and in which the supreme social value is liberty.

In its theoretical ideal, democracy, and particularly one focused on markets, is a minimal state. That is, individual interests are overriding. Happiness, satisfaction, and fulfillment must be sought for and can only be obtained by the individual in his or her own way, by reference to his or her own preferences, needs, and potentiality. The social well-being is simply the sum of individual satisfaction, and the social purpose is no more than the sum of individual purposes. Thus, democracy (emphasis on markets) cast on a liberal state has no purpose and no value other than to facilitate and protect the individual pursuit of personal values and private ends. In this view the state is subordinate to, and included only to protect the security and property of, the individual. For this purpose it lays down and enforces rules for the exercise of property power, lest the freedom of one transgress on the freedom of another. It must draw boundaries on the right of property, lest the claims of one trespass on the prerogatives of another, resulting in endless conflicts between ownership and ownership, between claim and claim. It must provide for the interpretation and enforcement of contracts entered into voluntarily by private parties in the process of exchanges.

Clearly, market democracy as a limited liberal state is primarily juridical.[5] It can do without an extensive and powerful bureaucracy. It cannot, however, do without a strong judiciary. It is a limited bureaucracy consisting primarily of judges, juries, prosecutors, and defenders, advocates representing interests before the bar, and police who enforce the rulings of the court.[6] It is essential to the operation of the market economy. The single skill appropriate to the bureaucrat is that of the lawyer.

By way of illustration, consider the American experience. The American state is basically judicial in character, and until the Great Depression, it was also a limited liberal state.[7] By constitutional fiat, as well as in practice, the American state did not have the autonomous power to intervene, control, plan, direct, or in any way significantly affect the cause of internal events or the structure of relationships, or the distribution of wealth and incomes, or the output of industry, or the character of like, or the nature of the economy.[8] According to this view, bureaucracy as such is singularly constrained in a strict support position to the fully acting, self-interested profit seeker.

The catastrophic collapse of the trading world during the period between the two world wars cast into doubt the viability of an essentially liberal state with its essentially juridical function. The Keynesian Revolution insisted that the economic system is not self-equilibrating and self-adjusting. Keynesians argued that the interwar economic collapse can be attributed to self-perpetuating insufficiency of aggregate expenditure. Hence, aggregate expenditures must be controlled and held at the level where labor would be fully employed. Only the state, in their view, has the power and responsibility to manage aggregate expenditures.

There is nothing new in the position that the state must bear responsibility for doing what the free market left undone. In fact, classical liberalism in the nineteenth century, with its strong bias against state intervention, nonetheless came to perform a host of functions—albeit to service local needs the market did not satisfy.[9] What is new is that the sovereign power of the state is called on by the Keynesian Revolution to manage an essential dimension of the entire economic system. The state must now stand responsible for the general level of unemployment of the country's human and physical resources. The juridical and defense function of the lawyer and soldier in the limited juridical state are now expanded to include the economist, whose prime task is to manage the country's aggregate spending. This joining of the new professional competence of the economist, the lawyer, and the soldier called forth an expanded state bureaucracy.

By way of contrast, the Marxist perception of the state and its bureaucracy has long remained a critique of capitalism without reference to the deep and both unresolved and resolved problems of early socialist regimes. These include (1) the reconciliation of the individual with collective values, (2) the organization of creative change, (3) the recruitment and selection of leadership, (4) the transference and control of power, and (5) the development of effective planning and rationale for collective choice.[10]

The classical Marxist conception of the state and its bureaucracy is that it serves to usher in and assure a classless communist society; once achieved, it would wither away. Following the Great Depression and World War II, Western capitalism did not follow Marxist predictions even though organized labor gained and maintained political control of the state and its bureaucracy. Neither private property nor the capitalist mode of production changed as a result of political control by labor. The growing intervention in the economy served to constrain laissez-faire liberalism and the operation of the market economy. The consequent emergence of the welfare state, which curbed capitalism and guaranteed the development of industrial trade unionism, transformed the state of the dominated classes. The net result has been to change the Marxist conception of the capitalist state as well.

The neo-Marxist theory of the state now views the capitalist state as functioning with the legitimacy of its authority based on universal suffrage. Thus, it does have the consent of the governed and the cooperation of the dominated, as well as dominating, classes. This is reinforced in part through income transfers and welfare guarantees that serve to satisfy the universal needs of all functional groups. The support is further buttressed through an apparatus of acculturation, socialization, and education, which instills ideologies of individualism and nationalism, and through the juridical system, which emphasizes values and focuses on private property rights and prerogatives. The net effect is to encourage the development of values stressing individualism rather than collective, group, or class values. The theory thus does not abandon the idea of the state as an instrument of class or the importance of the bureaucracy as its instrument.

Still another perception of bureaucracy is that of the nationalist state. A strict nationalist state typically finds its meaning in war or threat of war. It develops its strength, organizes all of its resources, and directs and controls the energies for its people in a perpetual readiness for, preparation for, or engagement in war. It is a maximal state and usually a military state as well. Its bureaucracy is well positioned to carry out the mandates of a nationalist state; and, of course, the bureaucracy also pushes nationalism for its purposes.

Thus, the nationalist state puts forth the idea of people who are one and indissoluble, who are banned together instinctively, who recognize their differences from all other people, and who are filled with a national spirit that gives to each a pride, a significance, and a meaning: in effect, one people, one bond, one law, one coin, one sovereign—and a bureaucracy to carry out its interests.

Nationalism represents a collective consumption good or public good whereby its consumption by one individual does not exclude its consumption by others.[11] The specific benefits of nationalism obviously go to those select nationals who acquire offices or property rights in which nationalism invests. This would include the bureaucracy, the elite, and producer interests. Due to the desire on the part of cultural, linguistic and communication interests to cultivate monopoly power, they are natural beneficiaries of a policy of nationalism, especially of its economic dimension.

If the demand by the elite and the bureaucracy for nationalism as a club good is added to the demand by the general population for nationalism as a public good, it is likely that there will be an overproduction of nationalism. This will tend to allocate too many resources for the creation and preservation of the nation-state, including a formidable bureaucracy and military. It is thus imperative that the bureaucracy and elite be discouraged and constrained from the use of nationalism to maximize their returns and advantages.

The growing role of government was not arrested in the postwar period, but was accelerated as a consequence of superpower tensions over basic political issues that quickly gained worldwide dimensions. In such an environment, new governments with a liberal orientation did not relinquish complete control of resources for production, research, and development to the civilian sector and the free market. Given the nature of the military and space demands for scientific input, it is unlikely that the civilian sector would have been able to meet these demands in any case.

These circumstances served to reinforce Keynesian ideas of managing aggregate expenditures by (1) encouraging/discouraging private investment through central bank manipulation of money supply and interest rates and (2) judicious budgeting of surplus/deficit at the source of public spending. The justification can be found in the Great Depression, which occurred as a consequence of a downward shift in aggregate spending (producing mass unemployment) because prices did not move freely. Prices neither registered scarcities nor equilibrated available resources to output preferences. Contrary to the neoclassical theory of prices, the evidence suggests (according to the Keynesian view) that prices are administered and controlled in modern industrial economies. Large corporations, unions, and other bureaucratic organizations—not a multitude of self-seeking individuals in competitive interaction—set prices. These organizations have the marketplace in which to set and administer prices. They are not answerable to a wider public, but only to their own constituencies. As a result, prices become a function of autonomous and arbitrary power that is neither answerable for its effects nor responsible for its consequences to society at large.

Efforts to monitor and control the exercise of arbitrary power on the part of these organizations increasingly push the government into the formation of prices and wages to ensure desired outcomes. This will typically lead to an increased role for the state bureaucracy to administer wage and price controls. Because wage and price controls inevitably fail, the system is increasingly driven into collective participatory planning, where wages and prices are determined—and, as we have discussed, this may, in fact, be desired by some people. Nevertheless, such an arrangement offers little chance that the market system, rather than a bureaucracy, will be allowed to play its effective and efficient role.

The net effects are an ever-increasing role and power for the state's bureaucracy, erosion of the market mechanism, and demoralization of its participants.

How can such a growing power be monitored and harnessed, or held accountable, or have its parameter fixed; or how could the electorate participate in the formulation of its policies? One way, of course, is for the state to undertake increasing supervision. However, this merely exacerbates the problem and follows the only too familiar sequence of having the state undertake more control and more complex responsibilities. In this sequence the issue for the individual ceases to be the liberty to choose and decide; rather, it becomes that of accepting whatever is decided on by the state and the bureaucracy.

Such activity by the state and its bureaucracy is no longer peripheral to and supportive of the operation of the competitive, price-directed market. Indeed, it casts aside the conception at the heart of neoclassical economics of a universe of individual self-seekers in competitive interaction, with resources and preferences optimally equilibrated by a free-moving price, mobilizing and allocating scarce goods and services. In its place comes the view of a world of large organizations, having enormous power to administer and control price as a function of organizational policy and being neither answerable to nor responsible die anyone other than those within the organization itself.

The exercise of autonomous and arbitrary power has also made useless much of the Keynesian prescription that was offered as a cure for capitalism's ills. The supportive manipulation of the money supply, interest rates, and aggregate spending in order to remove unemployment is absorbed by higher wages and higher prices, raised at their own initiative to benefit large organizations. This leaves unsolved the problem of general and specific unemployment. The state is left as the only agency capable of confronting the exercise of such power. As a most likely result, its own power would be increased at the additional expense of individual decision makers.

Perceptive scholars have long called attention to the emergence of a new class, which they have called bureaucratic and managerial. Neither capitalists nor workers were really running things. On the basis of expertise, a new group had insinuated itself into power everywhere. The enormity and complexity of the tasks facing contemporary society have served to promote the interests of this group.

These issues prompt scholars to devote their talents to determining what must be done to overhaul and direct the state and its bureaucracy to serve the desires and interests of its electorate. Intelligent and rational constraints must be designed against the exercise of arbitrary power by the state, its bureaucracy, and large autonomous organizations. It is counterproductive to heap abuse, contempt, and new tasks upon these bureaucracies without having a clear idea of what are and what are to be the rules for their behavior.

In another study, I have turned to cooperation theory, the theory of public choice, and economics for helpful insights into bureaucratic and political behavior.[12] According to public choice theory, politicians and bureaucrats are just like other people: They are driven chiefly by egocentricity, not by altruism. For example, the theory teaches that because politicians respond to pressure groups and the desire to be re-elected, the actions of government will often create or magnify market imperfections rather than overcome them. Thus, proponents of the theory tend to argue that the actions of government should be limited. Accordingly, public choice theorists advocate (1) a constitutional amendment to require a balanced budget, (2) deregulation, and (3) as recommended in this chapter, a system of well-defined guides within a lawful policy system of rules to constrain the exercise of preference by monetary authority for discretionary monetary policy.

Not everyone, of course, is prepared to accept the implications of the economic model for the behavior of the bureaucracy and the political elite. In particular, many are unprepared to accept the constraints on discretionary decision making by the bureaucracy. They argue that impediments such as distinguishing facts from values, the ambiguous nature of goals, and the pressures and costs of information cast doubt on constraining the exercise of discretionary authority. In any case, some argue, goals cannot and should not be agreed on in advance of decisions.

Moreover, critics note that political and economic choices are often conceived in different terms and are directed toward fulfilling different kinds of objections; therefore, they should be evaluated by different criteria. Some observers suggest that in a political setting a bureaucracy's need for political support assumes central importance, and that political costs and decisions are crucial. These costs and benefits, however, are difficult to measure and quantify. Political benefits that might accrue to a bureaucracy may be evident enough: for instance, obtaining short-term policy rewards and gaining enhanced power over future decisions. Political costs might be less obvious and might need explicit categorization.

It is also possible, as some observers note, that bureaucracies tend to behave for political reasons. Anthony Downs, for instance, describes a group of decision makers as "conservers" whose cautious behavior, minimizing individual or institutional risks, is inherently political.[13] Motives of self-interest, which Downs assigns to "clinchers" as well as to "conservers," are themselves political. "Mixed" motives of self-interest and altruism are also partly political. Only the primarily altruistic "statesman" seems to have the general good, not politics, in view. But, as Downs suggests, because the statesman does not compete for organizational resources, his function will simply be underfunded.

Most decisions, however they are measured, have political implications. The choice of criteria by which to measure decisional outcomes has political significance because of the possibility that adherence to a particular set of criteria will ultimately favor the political interest of one group over others. Caution must be exercised to avoid (1) the unthinking application of economic criteria to the measurement of political phenomena, and (2) the assumption that economic rationality is, by definition, superior to political rationality.

Advocates of political rationality defend it on these grounds: (1) One can accept propositions that politics are legitimately concerned with enabling the decisional processes of government to function adequately, (2) basing decisions on political grounds is as valid as basing them on other grounds, and (3) rationality according to the currency of politics is as defensible as rationality in economic terms. Properly conceived and applied political rationality can be a useful means for giving insight into bureaucratic processes.

Traditional conceptions of bureaucracy and its role in government are not accurate. These conceptions are, nevertheless, important in shaping views of bureaucracy. They include political neutrality in carrying out decisions of other government organizations; legislative intent as a principal guiding force for the actions of bureaucracy; legislative oversight of bureaucracy as a legitimate corollary to legislative intent; and direction by the chief executive—which, under separation of powers, creates the possibility of conflict over control of bureaucracy.

In the United States, moreover, significant problems arise from the fragmented nature of the various policy-making processes. The U.S. bureaucracy functions in a political environment where there is no central control over policy; as a result, considerable slack in the system allows the bureaucracy considerable discretion. Moreover, not all decision-making power or authority is clearly allocated; this results in many small conflicts over fragments of power. The net result is that bureaucrats in the United States are often active in political roles and take policy initiatives that are not neutral, thereby departing from traditional views about bureaucratic roles and functions. They are, in effect, in a position to develop semi-independence from elected leaders. Their activity, furthermore, is organized around jurisdiction over particular policy areas (e.g., the Federal Reserve Board, monetary policy, and banking). They make a special effort to prevent changes in jurisdiction that might affect their political interests or those of their supporters (e.g., the Federal Reserve Board and it relations with federal and local authorities who deal with monetary and banking affairs).

Bureaucratic power and accountability are major issues in contemporary society. Bureaucratic power is based in good measure on the ability (1) to build, retain, and mobilize political support for a given agency and its programs and (2) to make use of expertise in a particular field (e.g., monetary and banking affairs by the Federal Reserve Board). Bureaucratic accountability, especially in the United States, is difficult to enforce consistently and effectively because of frequently conflicting interests in the legislative and executive branches of government. The issue of accountability is made all the more difficult by the fact that U.S. bureaucracies operate under authority delegated by both the chief executive and legislative branch and with considerable discretion to make independent choices (again, consider the Federal Reserve Board and its relations with Congress and the executive branches of government).

THE JURIDICAL STATE

Democracy, and particularly market democracy in its theoretical ideal, is a minimal and primarily juridical state that has no value other than to facilitate and protect the individual pursuit of personal values and private ends. It is subordinate to, and intended only to protect the security and property of, the individual. For this purpose it lays down and enforces rules for the exercise of property power, lest the freedom of one transgress on the freedom of the another. It must draw boundaries on the rights of property, lest the claims of one trespass on the prerogatives of another. It must provide for the interpretation and enforcement of contracts voluntarily entered into by private parties in process of exchanges.

The concept of property rights typically involves various rights that are put together in a market democracy. These include the right to use property for personal use, including consumption and production; the right to receive proceeds from property rental; and the right to sell fixed and variable equity shares in an established enterprise.[14] These rights are promoted from theory to practice by contractual freedom within an environment that facilitates and protects the individual pursuit of personal values and individual ends. They characterize and describe the juridical nature of a market democracy.

A society's property rights are important determinants in wealth distribution. Historical evidence shows that some property rights promote growth and others lead to stagnation. However, little is known about the process by which property rights are established or how they change in response to new conditions. Studies—some serious, some otherwise—have examined the meaning of ownership and control, concepts that are so critical to the issue of property and their evolution over time and to changing conditions.[15]

NOTES

1. See Milton Friedman and Rose Friedman, *Free to Choose* (New York: Avon Books, 1981) and Milton Friedman and Rose Friedman, *Tyranny of the Status Quo* (Orlando, FL: Harcourt, Brace Jovanovich, 1984). See also George Macesich, *Money and Democracy* (New York: Praeger, 1990) and George Macesich, *Reform and Market Democracy* (New York: Praeger, 1991) and the studies and evidence cited there.

2. Alexis de Tocqueville, *Democracy in America* (Garden City, NY: Doubleday, 1969).

3. Harry Johnson, "The Ideology of Economic Policy in the New States," in D. Wall, ed., *Chicago Essays on Economic Development* (Chicago: University of Chicago Press, 1972), pp. 23–40.

4. See George Macesich, *The International Monetary Economy and the Third World* (New York: Praeger, 1981), Chapters 1 and 2.

5. Robert A. Solo, *The Positive State* (Cincinnati: South-Western Publishing Company, 1982), p. 57, and M. M. Clark, *Social Control of Business*, 2d ed. (New York: McGraw-Hill, 1939), pp. 95–96.

6. Solo, *Positive State*, p. 57.

7. Ibid., p. 59.

8. Ibid., p. 59.

9. George Macesich, *The Politics of Monetarism: Its Historical and Institutional Development* (Totowa, NJ: Rowman and Allanheld, 1984) pp. 16–38.

10. Robert A. Solo, "The Neo-Marxist Theory of the State," *Journal of Economic Issues,* 12:4 (December 1978), pp. 829–842.

11. George Macesich, *Economic Nationalism and Stability* (Westport, CT: Praeger, 1995), especially Chapter 2.

12. George Macesich, *Monetary Reform and Cooperation Theory* (Westport, CT: Praeger, 1989).

13. Anthony Downs, *Inside Bureaucracy* (Boston: Little, Brown, 1967), Chapter 8.

14. For a useful summary of issues involving property rights, see Harold Demsetz, "Towards a Theory of Property Rights," *American Economic Review* (May 1967), pp. 347–359; Marshall R. Colberg, "Property Rights and Motivation," *Proceedings and Reports,* Center for Yugoslav-American Studies, Research and Exchanges, The Florida State University, Vols. 12–13 (1978–1979), pp. 52–58.

15. See, for instance, "Capitalism: Survey," *The Economist* (May 5, 1990), pp. 5–20.

Chapter 5

The Monetary and Financial Organization: In Search of a Monetary Regime

PARADIGM ISSUE

Monetary authorities and central banks have pursued a number of economic goals: price stability, full employment, exchange rate stability, and balanced trade. The lessons from the 1970s, 1980s, and into the 1990s have led monetary authorities to believe that their primary goal should be price stability.[1] These lessons are empirical as well as theoretical.

From the early post–World War II years to the mid-1970s, there was almost a consensus among economists called the neo-classical synthesis. Because of serious theoretical problems, however, this paradigm broke down in the mid-1970s.[2] Attempts by economists to repair it have not been successful thus far.

The neoclassical synthesis drew from what many economists considered to be both valuable and useful—a combination of both classical and Keynesian economics. The classical contribution was the methodology derived from the propositions that consumers and producers are rational and that markets are such that prices adjust to maintain a balance of supply and demand. That unemployment of resources, which may not be voluntary, does exist is unexplainable in classical economic terms. The paradigm drew on the Keynesian contribution of "sticky prices," which means that prices and especially wages move sluggishly.

The paradigm thus proposed that consumers and producers are rational in their pursuit of self-interest and that markets do provide useful insights into the operation of an economy. Keynesians readily accepted the classical view. However, they added to it their own view that slowly changing prices are important to the way our economy behaves, particularly in the short run. Thus, in the long run the economy looks classical; whereas in the short run, if the economy is plagued by unemployment of its resources, the Keynesian description appears more realistic. Putting together the classical view with the Keynesian short-run view yielded the neoclassical synthesis.

During the late 1960s and into the 1970s, however, world economies began to produce results that did not conform with the neoclassical paradigm and became more and more skeptical about the forecasts the paradigm produced.

In particular, doubt was cast on the predictions derived from the large econometric models of the 1960s and the statistical relationship summarized in the Phillips curve (that unemployment went hand in hand with high inflation and vice versa). The theoretical framework (as summarized in the IS-LM framework) does provide that a rise in prices could lower real wages, temporarily raising employment and output. Together with the statistical relationship summarized in the Phillips curve, it is possible that rising prices or inflation could boost employment and output. This is the well-known trade-off between inflation and unemployment, which governments had been urged to watch closely. Any attempts at price stability policy then had to take advantage of the apparent inflation—an output trade-off.

It turned out, however, that the trade-off issue was illusory. In 1968, Milton Friedman looked into its theoretical microeconomic underpinnings, as did Edmund Phelps. The results for the trade-off issue were not encouraging. For the sake of argument, suppose it is true that inflation reduces real wages, and thus the demand for labor increases. The supply of labor may not be as forthcoming if workers are unwilling to supply as much labor as before. As a result, the increased demand for labor may not lead to increased employment. It may be that workers are mistaken about real wages and do not understand that a rise in general prices reduced their real wages and that a stronger demand for labor will increase employment. However, for the Phillips curve to hold, workers must keep making the same mistake. This is highly unlikely. For example, it would mean that if inflation had been averaging 8 percent per year, workers would need to keep on expecting prices to be stable next year; otherwise they would insist on recouping their real wage cut by demanding higher money wages.

This is not a realistic view of the world from the viewpoint of most people. It is not likely that inflation under such circumstances would come as a surprise. For such an event, inflation must be accelerating. There then might be a trade-off between inflation and output. This is likely to be transitory, however, and as people learn to anticipate stable inflation, so too will they learn to anticipate accelerating inflation.

In effect, a Phillips curve exists briefly where people's expectations are upset by surprise. If inflation is fully expected, there is no trade-off between inflation and employment. These events are summarized in the now familiar expectations-augmented Phillips curve.

The events of the 1970s, high inflation, and high unemployment—which the former Phillips curve analysis rejected—came as a sobering reality for the neoclassical synthesis. Thus, the postwar paradigm collapsed and with it its underlying consensus.

Many observers have noted that it may be politically difficult for monetary authorities to aim only at price stability while ignoring the unemployment rate. The Bush administration roundly criticized the Federal Reserve authorities for worrying too much about inflation in 1989, even though the unemployment rate was low at the time. It should come as no surprise that political pressure to stabilize the economy may increase in the event of disturbances from various domestic and/or international areas. If policy makers are forced to try to stabilize the economy, they would be well advised to remember that monetary policy has only a temporary effect on real variables, but a lasting effect on prices.

Since the 1970s, an economic and political search has gone on for a replacement paradigm. In the spirit of Friedman's challenge, one group has promoted a view based on the assumption that markets clear. The approach is usually called the New Classical School. Another group has challenged the market-clearing assumption but nevertheless has explored the microeconomic causes of market failure. This group is now called the New Keynesian School.

The breakdown of the postwar consensus has also served to usher in various disputes, some already simmering. Economic forecasting based on a large macroeconometric model has fallen into academic disrepute. Some theorists have been unwilling to cast their ideas in terms of the former paradigm. Other areas of economics have also come in for new emphasis. Thus, the focus on microeconomic foundations and the emphasis on extremely sophisticated mathematical techniques has brought with it new problems for both economists and politicians alike. Economists have become less sure of their ability to meet these challenges. Politicians have cast about for a new theoretical edifice on which to hang their programs.

Important elements in this new theoretical edifice, particularly for policy purposes, are the credibility and cooperation of the politicians and bureaucrats responsible for domestic and international economic policies, including monetary policy in particular. There is good reason to believe that the interwar consensus on economic policy collapsed from a lack of these two elements, which served to reinforce the shortcomings of the neoclassical paradigm.

DISCRETION VERSUS RULES: A FIDUCIARY REGIME

The collapse of the interwar consensus underscored both that central banks cannot fine-tune real economic growth and that in doing so they may jeopardize the goal of price stability. In their eagerness to boost growth and so keep politicians happy, many central banks, including the Federal Reserve System, with its anti-inflation policy, often lack credibility. In the American case, the blame lies primarily with Congress for giving the Federal Reserve the contradictory goals of promoting growth and reducing inflation.

There is support for the view that price level stability, popularly called *zero inflation*, is superior to inflation rate stability.[3] A contrary view is that the benefits of being at zero inflation are small compared to the costs of getting there and that most of the costs associated with nonzero average rates of inflation can be adequately addressed by adopting institutional changes that do not require specific inflation targets.

Most economists think that reducing price level uncertainty is a desirable objective despite the apparent lack of evidence that such uncertainty has important social welfare costs. It is the long-run uncertainty of inflation that most economists are concerned with and that makes the goal of zero price inflation so attractive to many of them.

In effect, the essential issue now for skeptics of price stability is that some type of rule is more desirable than none, including one for a specific low inflation rate that would eliminate the distortions currently induced by uncertainty about future policy and future inflation trends. Moreover, the essence of a policy is that it is a predictable response of the government or the central bank to a particular set of circumstances. Since it is not possible for a central bank to pursue a policy that consistently surprises people, some explicit arrangement must be put in place for monetary authorities to follow. Such an arrangement constitutes the country's *monetary regime*.[4]

A central problem in monetary policy is the issue of predictability and flexibility. How much discretion is to be granted monetary authorities over the formulation and execution of monetary policy depends on the monetary regime under which a country operates. Choosing an appropriate monetary regime for a country is critical if the credibility of monetary authorities is to be sustained.

The issue confronting policy makers and the public is whether monetary policy should be conducted within a rules-based system or according to the discretion of monetary authorities, including central bankers. This is an ongoing debate that goes back many years.

The debate itself has focused on three main reasons for constraining monetary authorities within a rules-based regime. The first reason, argued by Milton Friedman, is that monetary authorities simply lack knowledge and information that could produce a successful discretionary policy. Long and variable time lags in the effects on the monetary policy changes make discretionary fine-tuning a risky business indeed. There is no way to be confident that discretionary fine-tuning will in fact stabilize the economy. It may cause greater instability. For these reasons, Milton Friedman has recommended rules for a constant rate of growth in the money supply.

The second reason for shunning discretionary monetary authority in favor of a rules-based one is provided by economists working within the area of rational expectations. They argue that changes in monetary policy have no effect on the course of real economic activity, including employment. People simply take into account policy changes in forming their inflationary expectations. Thus, monetary expansion leads people to expect higher inflation, which then leads them to demand higher wages, thereby leaving output and employment unchanged. If this is the best that monetary authorities can do, so the argument goes, then they may as well operate within a rules-based policy regime, such as mandating a constant growth in the money supply, which at least minimizes the uncertainty about inflation.

Finally, the third argument is that a rules-based authority fosters the credibility needed to get around the so-called problem of time inconsistency. If a monetary policy appears optimal today, but tomorrow, when the time comes for monetary authorities to act on it, it does not, then without a rules-based policy regime, there is nothing to prevent the authorities from exercising their discretionary power and switching to what appears to be a better policy. If people believe that there is nothing binding the authorities to the original policy, they may behave in ways likely to prevent the monetary authorities from achieving their original goal. Thus, the need arises for a system of rules that everyone believes the monetary authorities will abide by. It is not so much the exact nature of the rules that is important as it is the need to establish a credible commitment from monetary authorities to follow those rules.

Consider now some of the major points raised by critics against monetary rules.[5] Two major points in dispute are, first, the concept of money and, second, the mechanism that links monetary and other economic variables.

The debate over the definition of money includes the issues of what is to be regarded as money now and the changing "moneyness" or liquidity of assets, because a fixed rule freezes the definition over time. The first issue is debated not only between advocates of and opponents to rules, but also within each group and among monetary economists in general. Various concepts of money have been defined, and most advocates of rules believe that a rule applied to any definition is preferable to the existing degree of discretion. Thus, it seems that the definition of money per se is not really a vital issue in the theoretical debate. The issue of the flexibility over time of the concept of money may be more important, but it is obviously also a matter of the degree of specific flexibility built into the rule. No proposal is regarded as final by various participants and observers of monetary policy in action.

The link between the stock of money and income is discussed in the velocity of money and, more specifically, in the variability or stability of velocity. Proponents of rules believe in a relatively stable and predictable velocity, whereas opponents tend to regard velocity as subject to erratic variations. Without analyzing all the details and individual differences, suffice it to say that these differences are no longer as sharp as they were.

A similar statement could be made about time lags, wherein the concern centers on three elements: (1) definition or measurement of lags, (2) their length or distribution, and (3) their variability. Typically, long and variable lags are associated with proponents of rules, whereas short lags are associated with opponents to rules. Friedman is the only one among the proponents who makes explicit allowance for the variability of lags. While a few proponents seem to share the belief in at least the possibility of relatively long lags, any dividing line, if it is to be drawn, does not follow the established rules-versus-discretion discussion. The haziness appears to be mainly a consequence of the lack of definitude in the theoretical issues.

Although the control of the stock of money under the present system is subject to adequate forecasting by the Federal Reserve, the issue of effective control is not restricted to monetary rules. After the money supply is accepted as an indicator or subtarget, any rational monetary policy implies effective control of the money supply as a prerequisite. Whether the present Federal Reserve System complies with this prerequisite is therefore a broader, much more basic question of monetary policy.

The essence of the differences between critics and proponents of monetary rules can be cast as another question: Can the target(s) be achieved more effectively and precisely by rules or by discretion? Two specific arguments can be usefully noted. The first is the often-heard critique that monetary rules are characterized by the implicit precept to ignore fiscal policy. The second is that the obstacle to rules is that several ends are in complex and unstable rivalry or conflict with each other.

The first argument appears overdrawn. Proponents of rules simply do not ignore fiscal policy. Whereas quite a few supporters rely more heavily on monetary policy, this cannot be interpreted as a subscription that only money matters. Whether or not money in fact matters the object should be to make money behave in the manner most consistent with economic stability.

The second argument implies the hypothesis that conflicting objectives can be served more effectively by a monetary authority that is to use its best judgment each time a decision of some sort is called for regarding the relative weight given to the objectives. Aside from the question of whether this kind and degree of discretion is compatible with the economic and political system, the intuitive nature of the argument hinges on another, more institutional, issue—the relative fallibility or infallibility of the monetary authority.

A GOLD STANDARD REGIME

It is obvious from American nineteenth-century experience that the gold standard provides a rules-based regime that can constrain the exercise of discretionary authority. It is also obvious that the domestic and international operation of such a set of rules requires commitment from both forms. In the years since World War I, however, this has not been the case.

Available evidence appears to suggest that economic performance in Great Britain and the United States was better under the classical gold standard than it has been under the managed fiduciary standard. For example, both price levels and real economic activity were more stable in the pre-1914 period under the gold standard than they have been in any period since. Accounting for much of the characteristically poor performance of this period was the unfortunate coincidence of troubles that produced the collapse of the international monetary and financial framework, as well as the subsequent deflation, real output instability, and high unemployment.[6] These results underscore the profound political, philosophical, economic, and social changes that have occurred in the world since the early years of the twentieth century.

According to M. D. Bordo, during the period 1834–1913, there was a slight downward trend in price levels on the average of 0.14 percent per year.[7] The exceptions to this trend were the sharp price rises during the 1830s, when substantial capital imports into the United States occurred, and the price rises again from 1861 to 1866 during the American Civil War, when the United States was off the gold standard. The rapid price deflation from 1869 to 1890 was necessitated in the first instance by the American return to the gold standard in 1879.

In the period since World War I, price stability has not been at all characteristic. In fact, in the United Kingdom, the United States, and elsewhere, price levels have been rising on the average. Short periods of price stability have occurred only during the 1920s under the Gold Exchange Standard, during the 1950s, and during the early 1960s under the Breton Woods System. From 1914 to 1979, price levels in the United States registered an annual increase of 2.2 percent, and in the United Kingdom they averaged an annual increase of 3.81 percent.

The overall record, then, indicates more long-term price stability during the gold standard era than in the years since departure from that standard. The tendency for price levels to revert toward long-run stable value under the gold standard ensured a measure of predictability with respect to the value of money. There could be short-term prices rises or declines; however, inflation or deflation would not continue.

Long-term price stability encouraged people to enter into contract with the expectation that changes in prices for commodities and production factors would reflect real changes, not changes in the value of money brought about by inflation or deflation. One consequence of the departure from the gold standard and the lack of constraint in general prices was to generate confusion (e.g., between changes in price leads and changes in relative prices). This confusion increased the possibility for people to misjudge signals and thereby to incur major economic losses.

The evidence in real per capita income for both the United States and the United Kingdom suggests that it too was more stable under the gold standard than it had been in any period since World War I. In the United States, the mean absolute values of percentage deviations of real per capita income were 6.64 percent from 1879 to 1913 and 8.97 percent from 1919 to 1979, excluding 1941–1945. For the United Kingdom the figures were 2.14 percent from 1870 to 1913 and 3.75 percent from 1919 to 1979, excluding 1939–45. Moreover, in the United Kingdom there was a permanent break in trend in 1919, so that in subsequent years real per capita income was almost always below trend.

Unemployment, too, was on average lower in both the United States and the United Kingdom in the pre-1914 period than in the post–World War I period. In the United States, the average unemployment rate for the period 1890–1919 was 6.78 percent, and for the period 1919–79, excluding 1941–45, it was 7.46 percent.

In the United Kingdom, the average unemployment rate over the period 1888–1913 was 4.30 percent, and for the period 1919–79, excluding the World War II years, 1939–45, it was 6.42 percent.

The evidence tends to support the view that the classical gold standard is associated with more economic stability than the managed fiduciary standard by which it was replaced. The problem with the comparison is that it includes the interwar period when the international monetary and financial organizations collapsed.

The evidence presented by Bordo takes this into account. Accordingly, three time periods were compared: the pre–World War I gold standard period, the interwar period, and the post–World War II period. The war years themselves were omitted for comparison. Overall, prices were more variable under the gold standard than in both post–gold standard periods. The least variability occurred in the post–World War II period. For the United States, the average annual percentage change in prices for the period 1879–1913 was 0.1 percent, and the coefficient of variation of annual percentage changes in the price level was 17.0. For the United Kingdom, during the period 1870–1913, prices shifted downward at an annual percentage change of minus 0.7 percent and a coefficient of variation of 14.9. For the period 1919–40, the United States recorded an annual percentage change in price of 2.5 percent with a coefficient of variation of minus 5.2. For the United Kingdom and the period 1919–1938, the average annual percentage change in prices was minus 4.6 percent with a coefficient of variation of 3.8. The post–World War II years (1946–79) for the United States showed an average annual percentage rise in the price level of 2.8 percent with a coefficient of variation of 1.3. During the same period for the United Kingdom, the average annual percentage rise in prices was 5.6 percent with a coefficient of variation of 1.2.

The stability of real output is suggested by the coefficient of variation of year-to-year percentage changes in real per capita output. The evidence for the United States suggests a coefficient of variation of 3.5 for the period 1879–1913; 5.5 for the period 1919–40; and 1.6 for the period 1946–79. For the United Kingdom, this coefficient is 2.5 for the period 1870–1913; 4.9 for the period 1919–38; and 1.4 for the period 1946–79.

In sum, real output was considerably less stable in both countries during the interwar years than during the post–World War II years, when both higher rates of inflation and lower variability in output and unemployment were registered. This demonstrates the apparent policy preference away from long-term price stability toward full employment and suggests the reason behind the strong inflationary pressures in the postwar years. It is on the basis of such evidence that the public recognized that a specie or gold standard monetary regime no longer existed and began to arrange its affairs accordingly.

The evidence also suggested that a fiduciary monetary regime based on a monetary rule for steady monetary growth could provide the benefits of the gold standard without its costs. A prerequisite for success, however, was a firm commitment from the government to maintain a monetary rule and to incorporate long-run stability as one of its goals.

In any case, the international gold standard or regime cannot now be restored. It requires a return to a set of economic, political, and philosophical beliefs on which that standard was based, which is unlikely. It is probably easier to deprive the government of its monopoly over money, although the magnitude of such a task should not be minimized. Because the sensitive issue of national sovereignty is involved, as well as for other reasons, governments will not voluntarily abdicate their power over money. Therefore, these difficulties permit an alternative approach in the form of constitutional monetary constraints designed to restrict government manipulation of the money supply.

WHAT IS TO BE DONE?

Constraints imposed on national monetary sovereignty by the rules of the international gold standard or regime have been eroding since the collapse of the international monetary system. Fumbling attempts to reimpose monetary constraints through international monetary reform since World War I have only served the cause of discretionary intervention and imposed tasks on the monetary system which that has been unable to attain.

Attempts to reimpose monetary constraint have not been successful because the contemporary world differs radically from the pre–World War I era. The revolutions of the nineteenth century were arrived at, assuring political and economic liberty, by breaking through the outworn controls of the preceding age of regulations. For the most part, the revolutions of our own time have been protests against the philosophy and institutions of the system of individualism based on natural rights. They have aimed at the opposite values of social control, and they have created myths and utopias of individual liberty. The impersonal forces of the market on which classical (and neoclassical) economists have relied to bring about a maximum of production and maintain high production tend now to be displaced as political ideals by objectives such as full employment and various social safety-net programs.

Inevitably, these objectives imply intervention and regulation. The only mechanism presently available for this is the national state and its bureaucracy, including the central bank. As we know, the penchant of bureaucracies for discretionary authority as a means of self-preservation and expansion is very strong. Nowhere is this more conclusive than in the expanded activities of central banks in domestic and international monetary affairs. Intervention and regulation, however, can take place within constrained policy systems. It does not necessarily call for the granting of important discretionary authority to the state bureaucracy, although extension of intervention has also prevented discretionary authority.

Few monetary problems have ever been so ingeniously contrived to maximize difficulty as that of granting discretionary authority to central banks. Such authority, when granted to central banks over domestic monetary policies—undertaken for various and often illusive goals—constitutes a formidable reinforcement of nationalism in the economic sphere and creates an important source of instability. At the same time, the discretionary authority serves the central bank well, whose preference function may indeed differ significantly from that of the general public. Central banks are an economic arm of the political interventionist position while admirably serving their own bureaucratic goals and interests.

Central banks are subject to political pressures, and their typical response, in the absence of explicit constraints, is to manipulate money and monetary policy as a matter of bureaucratic survival. They are, after all, creatures of the national state. Their independence is more myth than fact. Their alliance with political elements in government is understandable, as our theory of bureaucracy suggests. However, their attempts, through the exercise of discretionary policies to carry out the various goals assigned—for example, low interest rates, price stability, economic growth, employment, and balance-of-payments equilibrium—are more likely to cast doubt on both their own credibility and that of money and the monetary system itself. In fact, this is what has happened in the United States and elsewhere. Subsequent demands for monetary constraints and reform are thus understandable. Whatever may be thought of the wisdom or practicability of such intervention and use of discretionary authority by central banks, it must be recognized that the nineteenth-century integration of market processes has been impaired by the emergence in every country of a greater measure of state intervention, particularly in monetary affairs. Indeed, Milton Friedman and Anna J. Schwartz report at least between the 1930s and late 1960s and likely since the 1960s and into the 1990s, government intervention into foreign exchange and other markets has not served well the stated objectives of stability.

Recognition by the public of these drastic changes in the monetary regime or system from a largely constrained specie or gold standard regime to an unconstrained fiduciary regime has been slow. Since the mid-1960s, however, a pronounced awareness of these changes has been demonstrated by both lenders and borrowers alike.

Alarm and concern over the drastic changes in the monetary regime has prompted a variety of reform measures, ranging from proposals to impose constraints on the monetary regime within prescribed policy guidelines to calls for reinstituting interest rates and its concern with credit market conditions as guides to policy reminiscent of the banking school. Many such proposals have been taken from the dustbins of history with little if any modification.

Money and the monetary regime, however, are not a junkyard of political and economic system parts. These institutions have evolved along with the general economic and political economies. Attempts to resurrect defunct bits and pieces of outmoded systems to shore up or reform the monetary system are exercises in pure futility. The pre-Socratic philosopher Heraclitus summed it up well with his remark that we cannot step into the same river twice.

NOTES

1. See, for instance, *Monetary Policy Issues in the 1990s,* a Symposium Sponsored by the Federal Reserve Bank of Kansas City, Jackson Hole, Wyoming, August 30–September 1, 1989 (Kansas City: Federal Reserve Bank of Kansas City, 1989).

2. George Macesich, *Monetary Policy and Politics* (Westport, CT: Praeger, 1992).

3. See, for example, the exchange between W. Lee Hoskins, "Defending Zero Inflation: All for Naught," Federal Reserve Bank of Minneapolis, *Quarterly Review* (Spring 1991), pp. 16–20; and S. Rao Aiyagarai, "Response to a Defense of Zero Inflation," Federal Reserve Bank of Minneapolis, *Quarterly Review* (Spring 1991), pp. 21–24; see also George Macesich, (Westport, CT: Praeger, 1992), Chapter 2.

4. See the discussions in Colin D. Campbell and William R. Dougan, eds., *Alternative Monetary Regimes* (Baltimore: The Johns Hopkins University Press, 1986). The discussion by Campbell and Dougan in Chapter 1 is particularly useful on the issue of monetary regimes.

5. See, for example, George Macesich, *Monetary Policy and Politics*, op. cit., pp. 43–44.

6. See Milton Friedman and Anna J. Schwartz, *A Monetary History of the United States, 1867–1960* (Princeton, NJ: Princeton University Press for the National Bureau of Economic Research, 1963); Milton Friedman and Anna J. Schwartz, *Monetary Trends in the United States and United Kingdom: Their Relation to Income, Prices and Interest Rates 1867–1975* (Chicago: University of Chicago Press, 1982); George Macesich, *The International Monetary Economy and the Third World* (New York: Praeger, 1981).

7. See M. D. Bordo, "The Classical Gold Standard: Source Lessons from Today," *Monthly Review,* Federal Reserve Bank of St. Louis (May 1981), pp. 2–17.

Chapter 6

Inflation and Unemployment: A Managed Monetary Standard

A MANAGED MONETARY STANDARD

In the previous chapter, our discussion focused on the possibilities of using monetary policy to control the unemployment rate. We noted the essential presumption that biased expectations are essential to any trade-off between inflation and unemployment. In effect, monetary authorities may well influence the unemployment rate if we assume that these authorities are only able to predict future price movements and the public cannot. The assumption of rationality on the part of the public lays to rest any such ability on the part of the monetary authorities.

If the monetary authorities use any specific model of expectations formation to derive the public's forecasts, such models will predict only as long as the monetary authorities continue to act in a way to create private unbiased forecasts. Thus, as soon as monetary authorities use the model to create consistently biased forecasts, rational individuals will soon correct their models to yield unbiased forecasts.

Clearly, the problem confronting the monetary authorities is that the use of disequilibrium price dynamics to influence the voluntary behavior of the public in such a way as to be detrimental to its self-interests will cause the national public to modify its behavior and so frustrate the policy efforts of the monetary authorities however socially desirable such policies may be.

Milton Friedman discusses the several stages through which professional views of the relation between inflation and unemployment have gone in the past several decades. In the first stage, a stable Phillips curve was accepted.[1] In the second stage, notes Friedman, came the introduction of inflation expectations, as a variable shifting the short-run Phillips curve, and of the natural rate of unemployment, as determining the location of a long-run Phillips curve. The third stage is the apparent positive relation between inflation and unemployment. Friedman argues persuasively that this last stage is more than coincidental.

The economics profession readily accepted the level of unemployment and the rate of inflation because, as Friedman notes, it appeared to fill a gap in Keynes's theoretical structure. It seemed to provide the missing equation in that structure. Due to Keynesian acceptance of a rigid absolute wage level and a nearly rigid absolute price determined essentially outside Keynes's model by institutional factors, changes in nominal aggregate demand registered almost entirely in output and hardly at all in prices.

In fact, in his search for a workable monetary standard, Keynes founded, in the *General Theory*, according to John R. Hicks, the labor standard and its dependence on society's sociopolitical processes.[2] Because of other things, this translated into a managed monetary standard and justification for its discretionary management by central monetary authorities composed of an enlightened elite.

Keynes's efforts were translated into a managed monetary standard and yielded readily to discretionary monetary manipulation by authorities. The consequent monetary uncertainty generated by such manipulation has had the effect, on balance, of casting doubt on the credibility of these authorities, their policies, and ultimately on the monetary regime itself. In the process, the long-term price level lost its anchor. These are only the more obvious unintended consequences of Keynes's efforts.

As a monetary economist, Keynes was looking for a monetary standard that could be workable. In the *Treatise on Money* (1930), he was critical of the restored gold standard in the post–World War I era. His criticism was directed toward attempts to make the gold standard work as it had been reinstituted. He was, however, as Hicks points out, seeking to make it work. By the 1930s and into World War II, he was still searching for a reformed monetary standard that would be workable, as we know from his work in the creation of the International Monetary Fund.

Where in relation to Keynes's search for a reformed monetary standard does his *General Theory* of 1936 stand? Certainly, the years when the book was being written were years of monetary upheaval. The monetary crisis was needed due to an inadequacy in the supply of base money, consisting of gold, as many economists during and since the crisis have argued. This is what Keynes was to call a rise in liquidity preference. In effect, there was not enough base money for the banking system to be able to come to the rescue. Subsequent devaluations of the pound sterling and dollar in 1931 and 1933, respectively, removed the monetary constraint against expansion, as John Hicks argues.

How far would be it safe to allow such an expansion to go? This was the point, argues Hicks,

> where the revolution in Keynes's own thinking occurred. It was here that he had to pass from consideration of the monetary system (the understanding of which he was a master) to considerations of the real

economy, which I fear must be recognized that he understood it less well. It is true that long before he wrote the *General Theory*, he had been turning that way. His *Treatise* (1930) had been narrowly money; it was concerned with price levels and with their variations, not with output and employment. But now before he finished the *Treatise*, he was claiming he knew how to 'conquer unemployment.' That the prescription he was offering in his 1928 pamphlets would have involved a devaluation of sterling is, one may be sure, a consequence he would not have refused.[3]

Keynes was, of course, aware that focusing on employment could be a dangerous target. Given the need between 1928 to 1938 "to conquer unemployment," he was willing to do so. He defined "full employment" as the maximum that could be reached by expansionary measures, even though some residue of unemployment would still be out of reach to such measures. Hicks calls unemployment curable along the lines suggested by Keynes as "Keynesian unemployment."

In working out his theory, Keynes was assisted by assuming that the level of wages is in practice rather rigid. This was not an assumption that he accepted only for the benefit of the *General Theory*. It is, in fact, a belief that goes back at least to 1925 and his attack on the British return to the gold standard of the old parity. Indeed, as Hicks writes, "it was in relation to then existing level of money wages that he was claiming that sterling, after April 1925, was overvalued. It is doubtless true that during the 1920s and 1930s, the wage level in Britain was becoming more 'sticky' in money terms. But, when one considers the great variations, both upward and downward that occurred in 1918–1921, to have laid such stress upon rigidity, when rigidity had set in so recently, does seem peculiar."[4]

The tasks for economists and economies become much easier if we assume that wages are not only constant but rigid. It must be supposed in the conditions of Keynesian unemployment that the wage level, as Hicks points out, must be rigid so it is unaffected by changes in other variables. Thus it is, argues Hicks, that "the Keynes model is not just formally expressed in wage units; it is on a labour standard. A labour standard expresses the value of money in terms of labour, just as the gold standard expressed it in terms of gold."[5]

Under the gold standard, central banks stood ready to exchange money for gold as long as their gold reserves lasted. Under normal conditions and with care, such conversions could continue without endangering the standard. The trouble with the labor standard, of course, is that it has no reserves. There is no bank, no authority that can guarantee the convertability of money and labor. It is for this reason, argues Hicks, that it is only a pseudo-standard. For it is the labor standard that is the "major weakness of the Keynes theory and of the policies that had been based on it."[6]

If the monetary system adjusts itself to the level of money wages as envisioned in the *General Theory*, then sociopolitical forces gain in power relative to economic forces. Among these forces are included, of course, unions. Others, as

Hicks underscores, include the behavior of prices of the goods on which wages are spent. Since it is real wages in which labor unions and their members are interested, we have the making of a vicious circle of rising prices and wages all too familiar in the postwar period. In addition, we have no anchor for the long-term price level.

The price level in the Keynesian theoretical apparatus is indeed determined outside the system, as Milton Friedman demonstrates in "A Theoretical Framework for Monetary Analysis."[7] Most economists, including monetarists and Keynesians, would accept Friedman's framework as ideologically neutral and thus useful in analyzing fluctuations in income and prices in a wide variety of institutional and sociopolitical arrangements.

Given that the price level is determined outside the Keynesian apparatus, as Friedman demonstrates, it is not surprising that prices are set or administered by the bargaining power of respective parties, such as unions, oligopolies, and other institutional arrangements that restrict price flexibility. Views attributing inflation to one or another variety of cost-push causes are a manifestation of the external determination of the price level.

A number of cost-push and administered price inflation theories are discussed in the literature.[8] I call these theories antitraditionalist or cost-pusher views. As discussed in the literature, Phillips curve contributions represent attempts, for the most part, to link real magnitudes and the rate of change in prices to their initial historically determined level.

If we assume, as do monetarists and the quantity theory, that the economy is operational at the full employment level of real income, the distinction between the Keynesian and quantity theory view is clear. That is, real income is determined outside the system by appending the Walrasian equation of general equilibrium to it and regarding them as independent equations defining the aggregates. Friedman notes that this is the essence of the so-called classical dichotomy. In effect, the division between consumption and investment and the real interest rate is determined in a Walrasian real system, one that admits of growth.

This suggests one reason why quantity theorists and monetarists focus on increases in aggregate demand and specifically in increases in the stock of money as primary causes of inflation. These theories are known in the literature as traditionalist, or demand-pull, theories. Since changes in aggregate demand can also be engineered by fiscal policy manipulation, some advocates of demand-pull inflation may not share the quantity theorist or monetarist conviction on the importance of the stock of money.

Thus, the key differences between the Keynesian view and monetarist view are that Keynesians argue that change in the quantity of money affects spending via an interest rate effect on spending; and the monetarist view underscores wealth in portfolios and then in final spending.

Neither the quantity theory nor the Keynesian income-expenditure theory model is satisfactory as a framework for short-run analysis. According to Friedman, this is so mainly because neither theory can explain (1) the short-run division of a change in nominal income between price and output, (2) the short-run adjustment of nominal income to change in autonomous variables, and (3) the transition between the short-run situation and a long-run equilibrium described essentially by the quantity theory model.[9]

Milton Friedman suggests another approach.[10] He draws on Irving Fisher's ideas on the nominal and real interest rates and Keynes's view that the current long-term market rate of interest is expected to prevail over a long period. The Keynes and Fisher synthesis is then integrated into a quantity theory model together with the empirical assumptions that the real income elasticity of demand for money is unity and that the difference between the anticipated real interest rate and the anticipated growth of real income is determined outside the system. The result is a monetary model in which the current income is related to current and prior quantities of money. This monetary model of nominal income, according to Friedman, corresponds to the broader framework implicit in much of the theoretical and empirical work that he and others have done in analyzing monetary experience in the shortrun and is consistent with many of the empirical findings produced in these studies.

The quantity theory of money is basically a theory of the demand for money. It is at its best when the demand for money is a stable function of a few key variables. For instance, its stability is important because it ensures that *mutatis mutandis*, inflationary pressures from a change in the supply of money are transmitted to the general level of prices.

MINIMUM WAGE: POLITICS INTO ECONOMICS

The Democrat and Republican debate over the minimum wage in 1996 is but one illustration of attempts through the political processes to administer prices—in this case, minimum wages. About 2 percent of America's 107 million workers in 1996 earned the minimum hourly wage of $4.25. An additional 9 percent earned between $4.25 and $5.15 an hour and so would also be affected directly by President Clinton's proposal to raise the minimum wage to $5.15 an hour. The typical worker in that pay range is a white woman over the age of 20. If the minimum wage is lifted, however, millions more would most likely see their wages rise as employers adjusted pay scales upward.

Under unrelenting pressure from Democrats and facing increasing clamor within his own party, Speaker of the House Newt Gingrich (R., Georgia) promised House Republicans, who support increasing the minimum wage, a vote in the issue in May 1996. Indeed, the minimum wage was last increased in 1989 when legislation was passed by an overwhelming majority and survived a veto by President Bush. In fact, informal surveys have shown that a majority of the members in both the House and Senate support an increase in the minimum wage.

The notable exception of prominent participants in the debate is Representative Dick Armey (R., Texas), a former economics professor and House majority leader. He ardently opposes an increase in the minimum wage for reasons based on sound economic analysis and apart from political appeal. One observer noted that in the spring of 1996, hardly a workday passed without Senator Tom Daschle of South Dakota, the minority leader, or some other Democrat speaking out on the wage issue on the Senate floor or trying to maneuver opposing Republicans into an embarrassing vote on raising the minimum wage.

Senator Bob Dole (R., Kansas), the Republican Party's 1996 Presidential nominee, had suggested that he would allow the minimum wage question to come to a vote in the Senate, possibly tied to a measure to reduce the federal tax on gasoline. In any event, it is generally agreed that both houses of Congress support an increase in the minimum wage, something President Clinton has been advocating.

The sad fact is that neither proposal makes much economic sense. Reducing gasoline taxes will make deficit reduction more difficult while encouraging increased consumption of gasoline. Raising minimum wages will throw some on low wages out of work. Neither will make much difference, for good or ill, to the American economy. Their importance stems purely from the fact that they are high-profile, voter-pleasing economic issues that politicians like to serve to the public.

Politics into economics simply will not go. By reducing the efficiency of the U.S. economy, these byproducts of political expediency will also reduce its real income. Disappointment with the economy's performance on this score increasingly pushes the government into the formation of prices and wages to assure desired outcomes. This will typically lead to price and wage controls. Since wage and price controls inevitably fail, the system is increasingly driven into collective participatory planning, in which wages and prices are determined. This may, in fact, be denied by some people. Nevertheless, such an arrangement offers little chance that the market system will be allowed to play its effective and efficient role.

The inevitable failure of price and wage controls is readily demonstrated by considering some problems and consequences of prices for individual products and services (including wages). The effects of a fixed price for a product or service depend in the first instance on the level at which it is fixed and whether it is a minimum or maximum price.

To illustrate the issues, let us suppose we set up an administrative agency to fix prices. Now suppose this agency fixed the price of a commodity or service precisely at the level at which it would fall relative to other prices if there were no price controls and the price were established by the market forces. In this case, the price control will have no effect, and our agency will have performed a needless exercise. Of course, the administrative costs incurred by this exercise will be borne by the taxpayer.

Now suppose that our agency sets a fixed price that is a maximum price, but that it sets the price at some level lower than what the price would be if it were determined by free market forces. In this case, shortages will appear. People will want to buy more of the commodity or service than they otherwise would, but less of the product or service will be produced than otherwise would have been produced. Why should less of the product be produced at this lower price? The reason is simply that at the lower price it becomes more profitable to produce other items whose prices are not fixed at this lower level. If more is demanded than is supplied, then some system determines who among the people is going to get the product or service in question. This can be accomplished by attaching another office to our price-administering agency, whose function will be to issue coupons, or the product or service can be given to old and regular customers of the suppliers, or it can be done according to the rule "first come, first served." This is, of course, the familiar case of the queue, with all the losses in time spent waiting one's turn.

If less of a product or service is produced because its price is fixed too low, it must be that fewer resources are employed. What happened to those resources? They simply moved to other industries producing products and services whose prices were not controlled. Ironically, since prices that tend to be controlled in essential industries are not controlled in inessential industries, price controls tend to cause fewer of the essential products or services to be produced and more of the unessential products or services.

The foregoing need not be the case at all, some will say, since the government can induce producers of the commodity or service in question to produce more at this lower price by offering them an incentive in the form of a subsidy. This means that, in effect, producers now receive a higher price, raised artificially by the government subsidy. The taxpayer in general will now bear not only the cost of the price-administering agency, but also the cost of the subsidy.

Consider our last case, in which a minimum price is fixed at a level higher than that which would prevail in a free market. Now there will be initial surpluses. At the higher price, the product or service will be produced. Instead of rationing consumers, it will now be necessary to ration the production of the product or service among the many producers who would be willing to produce at this higher price. Again, as in the case of consumers, this can be done by attaching an office to our price-administering agency, whose function will be to allocate by quota production of the product or service in question.

This, in general, is the all-too-familiar problem of U.S. agricultural surpluses. In this case, the taxpayer as a consumer will likely pay the higher price for the product or service as well as the cost of the administering agency.

Selective price controls, moreover, cannot avoid discrimination. If a producer's selling price is fixed, there is usually an obligation to control the producer's costs. This means fixing more than the prices of a producer's more obvious inputs, such as labor and raw materials. It also means that such items as taxes, interest costs, and business costs must also be fixed.

Control of labor costs, however, is most difficult. Elements of labor costs such as fringe benefits, compensation for overtime work, shift differentials and paid leave serve to complicate the already difficult task of setting wage rates. The U.S.

federal minimum wage example serves to illustrate the difficulties in setting wage rates.[11]

Based on economic theory, one would expect the inverse relation between changes in the minimum wage and substitution (capital for labor) effects to be confirmed. When information on evasion and violations of the minimum wage law is taken into account, considerable light is shed on the complexities of wage fixing. In effect, an increase in the minimum wage is equivalent to a reduction in the price of evasion and avoidance. The price of evasion and avoidance is the cost of evasion and avoidance minus the benefits of evasion and avoidance. The benefit has increased with the increase in the minimum wage. Other things being equal, one would expect evasion and avoidance of the minimum wage to increase. This also appears to be confirmed by the evidence.[12]

The minimum wage has had adverse effects on wage differentials, and these differentials serve a useful purpose in allocating labor services into various occupations.[13] They are, in fact, an essential part of the price mechanism. When they are subjected to an autonomous shock in the form of a government fiat, a compression of wage differentials occurs. The wages of those directly affected by the rise in the minimum wage rise more than wages of those not so directly affected. Since it is not as easy to allocate labor services as it is other services and goods, the problem of production adjustments is aggravated.

Matters are further complicated by difficulties in defining exactly what it is that is being controlled. Failure to specify accurately the end product or service leads to the inevitable tendency to increase profit margins by cutting quality, particularly where shortages already exist. The problem, moreover, is not simply one of quality deterioration. There is also the tendency for the variety of products to be reduced.

In the face of domestic price over wage ceilings, there is always the tendency for a producer to sell abroad at a higher price. When producers are allocated fewer productive resources than they desire, they may seek to increase their supply by imports. This inevitably leads to price controls and physical controls over imports, such as foreign exchange controls and import and export quotas. The general direction into which a country adopting such controls is pushed forces its government and bureaucracy into a position as the sole judge of the volume and direction new investment will take. Government (and, more specifically, its bureaucracy) dominates the field of new investment through its policies regarding profits and sales.

Even more important, perhaps, failure to allow the market system to play its effective and efficient role almost assumes that money and the monetary system will not be allowed to play a nondiscriminatory and autonomous role within the constraints of a rules-based policy system so necessary to assure the preservation of economic and monetary stability in the country.

UNIONS AND INFLATION: WAGE-COST-PRICE SPIRAL

There is a general agreement that workable solutions must be developed for the problems of contemporary society. A recurring public issue is the perceived responsibility of unions/and or labor for inflation. The issue turns on the so-called wage-price or cost-price inflation.

The reasoning underlying recovery of the inflation theories is based on the Keynesian tradition and may be summarized in the now familiar cost-price-spiral inflation. Although there are many variations on the theme, the common thread is the assertion that the pricing mechanism is becoming progressively less sensitive. Whatever the alleged cause of inflation, the monetary preconditions must be satisfied so that the distinction among theories in the Keynesian tradition is between different mechanisms of inflation. Three variations on the theme, however, appear sufficiently important from a public policy viewpoint to warrant consideration. One is that minor pressures for wage increases are the causal element in inflation. The second is that oligopolistic sectors administer prices and so are the causal elements in inflation. The third incorporates elements of the first two and tangentially places the blame for inflation on the existence of both unions and oligopolistic industries.

The first variation argues that unions are responsible for inflation in that they fail to recognize that wage increases that go beyond overall productivity gains are inconsistent with stable prices. Thus, the argument is that unions push up wages, which raises costs and prices. In order to avoid a logical fallacy, the more sophisticated argue that since the monetary authorities are committed to a policy of full employment, they will expand the money supply to make possible the sale of old output at the new price level.

The second variation argues that prices are set in a different way in those sectors of the economy that are composed of many firms than they are in industries where there are a few major producers. Prices set by oligopolistic industries are administered so that they are excellent conductors of inflationary pressure. They are relatively immune to traditional anti-inflationary policies in that their prices, having once reached a high level, are stickier in declining than those of competitive industries when demand declines.

The third variation claims that unions and oligopolistic industries are primarily responsible for inflation. Unions, so the argument goes, lodge themselves in oligopolistic industries and share in the "spoils" derived from the product side. Thus, unions in such industries may take advantage of the inelastic or expanding demand conditions on the product market to obtain higher wages without fear that the entry of new firms will reduce union wage gains. According to this variation, the product market permitting, the oligopolist will grant a higher wage rate as a means of avoiding a more costly strike. Moreover, in contradiction to more traditional views, such unions need not be old craft unions; they may be the new industrial unions that economists have tended to treat as relatively powerless in setting excessive wages. It is for this reason, presumably, that the advent of new industrial unions, when coupled with oligopolistic industries, has changed the American economic system so greatly as to frustrate attempts to control inflation along traditional lines. In effect, the argument implicitly assumes that the pricing mechanism is becoming progressively less fluid or automatic.

In place of traditional methods for coping with inflation, which some Keynesians consider largely ineffective or inappropriate, they advocate a direct assault on the problem of inflation. Although such an assault may take many forms, three seem to be dominant. First, government should resort to "moral suasion" to induce business and labor to exercise their power in a socially desirable (noninflationary) way. Second, government could increase the degree of competition in the marketplace by a more vigorous enforcement of antitrust legislation. Some people argue that since labor unions are monopolies, they should also be subject to antitrust legislation. Third, government can participate more actively in or control the price-and-wage-setting process. Needless to say, these forms of control are not mutually exclusive.

Eclectics view the discussion of whether inflation is demand pulled or cost pushed as analogous to "which came first, the chicken or the egg?" They attempt to synthesize, in varying degrees of sophistication, the two views of inflation. Of the several syntheses available, we shall consider only two. One, which draws heavily on the Keynesian tradition, turns on the assertion that we cannot empirically isolate inflation by types. The other, which draws heavily on the monetarist tradition, asserts that we cannot conceptually isolate inflation by types.

The synthesis that draws heavily on the Keynesian tradition asserts that it is impossible empirically to test for the existence of leads or lags from the cost or demand side, which is necessary if we are to classify inflation by types. For such a purpose, we need minute data on the cost and demand sides. Since such data presumably are not available, we cannot meaningfully classify inflation by types.

Even if such data were available, they would shed little light on the causes of inflation. Prices and wages, according to this view, are not set in the traditional manner. They are set with reference to some markup over the cost of living. Accordingly, inflation is generated whenever labor and management attempt to get more than 100 percent of the selling price. This is an impossible situation. Yet it is on the impossibility of the situation that the continuing process of inflation depends. Thus, each party increases the part it tries to take by increasing wages or by increasing prices. Since together they cannot succeed in getting more than 100 percent of the selling price, wages and prices are continually raised, thereby generating a continuing process of inflation. The process of inflation, though it may originate in the noncompetitive sector where market power is sufficient to raise prices and wages, will spill over into the competitive sectors, thereby gaining momentum.

This may occur, it is argued, either from the demand side or cost side, or both. Since the prices of the products and services of the noncompetitive sector rise, there will be a change in the composition of demand. Consumers will switch their demand to the products and services produced by the competitive sector so that prices rise in this sector. The deficiency of demand will result in some unemployment in the noncompetitive sector. Due to factor immobility, however, unemployment in this sector will not cause wages or prices to fall, so that unemployment persists. Attempts by the government to remove excess demand along traditional lines to check the overall price rise, while removing excess demand in the competitive sector, increase still further the unemployment in the noncompetitive sector.

The same situation will prevail even if the spillover occurs from the cost side. Thus, the spillover will occur because wage or price rises in the noncompetitive sector are signals for labor and employers in the competitive sector to do the same in order to protect, if not increase, their relative income shares. Accordingly, the government is confronted with the dilemma of either inflation or unemployment.

The other view, which borrows heavily from the traditional position, argues that we cannot even conceptually identify inflation by types, much less classify them empirically. In essence, this view turns on the proposition that while it is obvious that demand conditions influence costs, it is equally obvious that one cannot separate out the portion of the cost increase attributable to increased demand. Traditional monetarists and Keynesians accordingly have erred in attempting to establish rigid links between types of inflation and public policy.

The eclectic views essentially do not consider as practical the argument that the monetary authority, by refusing to expand the money supply, could "nip in the bud" an inflationary spiral. The bases for such an assertion are (1) that velocity would increase, thereby frustrating the efforts of the monetary authority; and (2) that even if velocity could no longer increase, the monetary authority could overcome the strong institutional forces making for rigidity in the pricing system only at the expense of a possible serious depression.

In order to control inflation, therefore, steps should be taken to remove institutional and other rigidities from within the American economic system. It is only then that the control of inflation along more traditional lines would have effect.

We may turn now to our appraisal of the aforementioned views of inflation by drawing both on economic theory and on recent experience. Theoretical and empirical evidence, though not completely inconsistent with alternative views, tends to support traditional monetarists' views of inflation.

The fundamental discovery of those deemphasizing the traditional view of inflation is that prices and wages go up when somebody raises them. There is general agreement regarding the facts. We take it to be true that most sellers would always like to raise their prices. We also take it to be true that sellers will never raise their prices without limit. What are the limits and circumstances under which sellers will raise their prices? It is precisely to the answering of this question that economists have directed their labors.

The fruit of this labor has produced the consensus that the state of demand will set the limit and the circumstances under which sellers can raise or lower prices. The state of demand permitting, sellers can raise their prices without being penalized by a loss of sales and income, and so they decide to raise prices. If, on the other hand, the state of demand permits a rise in prices only at the expense of losing net income, sellers will not raise prices. There is thus no conflict between the view that prices rise because somebody raises them and the view that somebody decides to raise prices because the state of demand permits such a rise without losing sales and income.

The views that deemphasize the traditional approach to inflation do not provide an alternative theory of inflation that is independent of the state of demand. Although not new, such views gained currency in the postwar period, when a favorable state of demand permitted price increases without the loss of incomes, and so sellers decided to raise prices. In effect, the decision to raise prices is simply the form whereby a disequilibrium situation was brought into balance. In the absence of a favorable state of demand, however, such a decision may result in distortions in the relative price structure, or a one-time increase in the general level of prices coupled with a loss of sales and increased unemployment. There is nothing in the process whereby sellers decide to raise prices that will assure a favorable state of demand. It is essentially for this reason that these views have descriptive but not analytical validity.

Consider the view that unions are responsible for inflation in that they push up wages. In support of this view, evidence is presented that unit labor costs (in money forms) have risen faster than average productivity. In a period of inflation, this observation is a truism. It does not help us to tell whether wages pushed up prices or demand pulled up wages.

Albert Rees pointed out long ago that in the absence of a favorable state of demand, unions can cause either shifts in the relative wage structure or a one-time increase in the general level of wages together with increased unemployment. The flexibility of nonunion wages determines what will occur. On the other hand, if the state of demand is favorable, union wage increases can be followed by inflation and continued full employment.

An important but unfortunately neglected point is that a necessary (but not sufficient) condition for unions to set off a wage-price spiral is that they need more power to raise wages: They must have increasing power to do so. This is a point argued by Milton Friedman more than thirty years ago and reported before the Industrial Research Association in 1959. In fact, there is little evidence that unions are becoming increasingly strong. Indeed, to judge from the size of union membership roles and recent unfavorable legislation, that power may be decreasing.

The aforementioned limitations similarly restrict the usefulness of the eclectic view that inflation is triggered and generated whenever labor and management attempt to get more than 100 percent of the selling price. It too depends on the existence or assurance of a favorable state of demand. At the same time, each party must be increasing its power as a necessary condition for setting off the wage-price spiral.

The positions that argue that union demands spill over into competitive sectors and so cause wages and prices to rise in this sector also depend, contrary to many of their adherents, on the existence of a favorable state of demand. This state of demand occurs when union employers bid away more and better workers from other employers and so lead these employers to raise wages in order to hold their employees. Again, there is no conflict between the view that wages and prices rise because somebody raises them and the view that somebody raises them because of a favorable state of demand for such a rise exists.

If this state of demand is not favorable to such a rise, a very different story will unfold and we may just as well talk in terms of a "spill-in" effect (movement of labor from union to nonunion activities). If, due to higher wages, union employers curtail employment, the movement in general wages will depend on two conditions. First, if wages elsewhere are flexible downward, the union workers will spill into nonunion activities and so nonunion wages will tend to fall. Second, the moment in the general level of wages, if any, will depend, as Albert Rees pointed out, onn the precise shapes of demand schedules of union and nonunion employers.

Consider now the view that oligopolies and monopolies, by administering prices, cause inflation. As noted elsewhere, the assertion is that administered prices are more rigid than competitive prices, and so they are excellent conductors of inflationary pressures.

Many economists (Martin Bailey, for instance), argue that administered prices are not as rigid as they seem. Insofar as these prices are rigid, their role in inflation is misunderstood. According to this interpretation, administered prices during periods when the state of demand is favorable do not rise as rapidly as competitive prices; so in effect, they may well be below levels that would clear the market, thereby creating waiting lists and grey markets. When administered prices do rise, however, they are apt to do so in large jumps, thereby attracting wide-spread attention and changes that are responsible for inflation.

The converse argument—that administered prices are rigid in the downward side and so respond more slowly to an unfavorable state of demand than competitive prices—also leaves much to be desired. In the first instance, the evidence used to support this assertion is far from conclusive. Thus, the usual American evidence cited is that after World War II, during periods (particularly 1957–58) when the state of demand was unfavorable, output and employment declined but prices, as judged by price indexes, did not. An examination of the past record, however, suggests that this is not a unique experience. Of the seven recessions since 1920 (other than 1957–58), in four of them the consumer price index rose in the early months. Furthermore, these price indexes, among other limitations, do not pick up price changes that take the form of special discounts or other informal price concessions, such as freight absorption or advertising allowances. The effect is an understatement of actual price changes, and an overstatement of the actual degree of rigidity. In the second instance, insofar as the administered price argument throws the blame for inflation on large corporations, available studies suggest little if any relation between concentration ratios and price rigidity.

In the view of many economists, the source of price rigidity is not the market sector of the economy but, ironically, the government sector. It is this sector that administers rigid prices through the medium of various regulatory agencies, price support programs, minimum wages, agricultural marketing programs, support of fair trade, and restrictions on both domestic and foreign trade. Such policies are largely inconsistent with attempts to remove monopoly elements from the economy.

According to the view that incorporates unions on the factor side and oligopolies on the product market side, large wage increases won by strategically placed unions may lead either to (1) distortion of the wage structure if other wages lag or (2) rising costs and upward pressure on prices if other wages rise equivalently, or a combination of the two. The net effect will be that the economy will move between episodes of price plateaus (accompanied by a stretching of the wage structure) succeeded by periods of rising prices.

But this view, as with others that deemphasize the traditional approach to inflation, contributes nothing essentially new to our understanding of inflation. The traditional view does not deny that unions may distort wages or that unions may share in monopoly spoils. As noted elsewhere, in the absence of a favorable state of demand, this may be one of the effects of a union wage rise. As the aforementioned view claims, the precise proportion between wage-distorting and cost-inflationary forces depends on the economic climate—in particular on the level of national income. It simply reasserts the traditional view with the emphasis on the favorable state of demand.

The interesting point about this view is the implicit assertion that new industrial mines and oligopolies have, apparently, sufficiently changed the economic structure so that the pricing system lacks fluidity. Little evidence other than a casual empiricism is offered in support of the aforementioned view. Indeed, such evidence as we do have supports the opposite view—that the pricing mechanism is not becoming progressively less sensitive.

Some consider the distinction between demand-pull and cost-push inflation useless. One view asserts that we cannot empirically identify inflation by types. This view apparently turns on the question of the timing of demand-pull and cost-push types of inflation (that is, on the identification of the lead and lag series). If the inflation of the demand-pull type, then presumably demand leads the increase in costs. If it is cost push, then costs should lead demand.

To make the distinction between the two types of inflation in this manner is to confuse the issue hopelessly. One would be hard put to identify the existence of leads and lags in the various relevant series. The consensus, however, seems to be that the essential difference between the two types of inflation is to be found not in the timing of the various series, but rather in their sensitivity to changes in demand.

Thus, if the struggle to obtain more than 100 percent of the selling price is sensitive to sales losses and unemployment, then it is unlikely that the struggle will continue in the absence of a favorable state of demand. On the other hand, if in the face of an unfavorable state of demand the struggle is such that substantial losses in sales and unemployment are the consequences, it does make sense to talk in terms of types of inflation.

Another view is that we cannot conceptually classify inflation by type. This view is interesting in that at times it is similar to the argument that raged in the latter part of the nineteenth century over the determination of value. The view states that we cannot identify that part of the price rise attributed to a cost increase and that part attributed to an increase in demand. The argument was settled, of course, when it occurred to economists that "each blade in a pair of scissors cuts." The analogy between the controversies breaks down because this view claims too much. Economists have long held that although each blade cuts, it makes sense to distinguish between the blades. Changes in the price level may occur with shifts in either the supply schedules or the demand schedules or both.

To argue that we cannot conceptually identify which part of a price rise is attributed to costs and which to demand is to assert that we are always in a position whereby both schedules shift simultaneously and by about the same amount. It would not be difficult to conjure up cases in which either demand or supply is the dominant element in price rises.

Although arguments against traditional methods of controlling inflation take many forms, they do possess a common thread: We cannot expect high levels of employment and output and at the same time maintain stability in the general level of prices. This is now the familiar unemployment versus inflation dilemma. Due to the lack of fluidity in the American pricing system, we cannot, so the argument goes, attempt seriously to use traditional methods against inflation because their use would simply add to unemployment. Inflation, accordingly, is the necessary price we must pay for avoiding unemployment and, presumably, for maintaining high levels of output.

This represents another aspect of inflation views drawing on the Keynesian tradition. It attempts to rationalize the relation of wage and price movements to aggregate demand and supply through the Phillips curve, which, as we noted, argues a link between variations in employment and price changes.

There are a number of reasons why the lack-of-pricing-fluidity argument falls short of providing an adequate explanation. In the first place, less than a third of workers are organized into unions, and many of these are weak unions. As Rees and others have noted, even a strong union may temper its wage demands when confronted with the existence or possibility of unemployment. Furthermore, the idea of the spillover effect, whereby unions set a pattern for wage demands for nonunionized workers, is not independent of demand. In the second place, the commitment by government to shore up the employment wall is not a commitment in particular occupations. Individuals and organizations are still free to price themselves out of the market. Finally, the argument tacitly assumes the existence of a period when prices and wages were flexible, and then proceeds to argue that the situation now has changed and prices and wages are no longer flexible—at least not in the downside. But we do not have studies that indicate that prices and wages were more flexible in the past than they are now. The studies that are available do not support the contention that the pricing mechanism is becoming progressively less sensitive; however, they do suggest continuing fluidity.

NOTES

1. Milton Friedman, "Nobel Lecture: Inflation and Unemployment," *Journal of Political Economy* 85:3 (June 1977), pp. 451–472.

2. John R. Hicks, "The Keynes Centenary: A Skeptical Follower," *The Economist*, June 8, 1983, pp. 17–19.

3. Ibid., p. 17.

4. Ibid., p. 18.

5. Ibid., p. 18.

6. Ibid., p. 18.

7. Milton Friedman, "A Theoretical Framework for Monetary Analysis," *Journal of Political Economy* (April/May 1970), pp. 193–238; Milton Friedman, "A Monetary Theory of National Income," *Journal of Political Economy* (April/May 1971), pp. 323–337. See also George Macesich, *Monetarism: Theory and Policy* (New York: Praeger, 1983), pp. 43–60.

8. See George Macesich, *Monetarism: Theory and Policy*, Chapter 7.

9. Friedman, "A Theoretical Framework for Monetary Analysis," *Journal of Political Economy* (April/May 1970), pp. 193–238.

10. Friedman, "A Monetary Theory of National Income," *Journal of Political Economy*, 1970, pp. 323–337.

11. See, for example, George Macesich and Charles T. Stewart, Jr., "Recent Department of Labor Studies of Minimum Wage Effects," *Southern Economic Journal* (April 1960); Marshall R. Colberg, "Minimum Wage Effects on Florida Economic Development," *Journal of Law and Economics* (October 1960), pp. 100–107.

12. Macesich and Stewart, "Recent Department of Labor Studies," pp. 288ff.

13. George Macesich, "Are Wage Differentials Resilient? An Empirical Test," *Southern Economic Journal* (April 1961), pp. 100–109.

Chapter 7

A Role for Fiscal Policy

THE RISE OF FISCAL POLICY

Economists usually define fiscal policy as the manipulation of government spending or taxes for the purpose of affecting aggregate demand. By fiscal policy multipliers, we mean ratios of the change in real gross national product to policy-induced changes.

Fiscal policy emerged as a response to the practical and theoretical problems of the 1930s. Before that decade, the maximum of sound government finance had been the balanced budget, balanced annually. This rule was coupled with another—a sound money system—which meant the gold standard and a central banking system that confined itself to maintaining a supply of money sufficient for the legitimate needs of trade.

The change from the old to the new fiscal policy came during the 1930s. In the early years of the Great Depression, the United States as well as other countries attempted to combat the Depression with cuts in government expenditures; by so doing, they may have made matters worse. Indeed, Franklin Delano Roosevelt campaigned in 1932 on promises to restore sound finance and a balanced budget in the orthodox tradition. Once in office, however, Roosevelt's policies included significant expenditures for public works and employment relief. At about the same time, John Maynard Keynes proposed deficit spending—that is, spending from borrowed funds—as a means for economic recovery in Great Britain. In 1936, when Keynes published *The General Theory of Employment, Interest, and Money*, the foundation for the modern theory of fiscal policy was laid. After several years of discussion and controversy, Keynes's theories came to be incorporated into the main body of accepted economic theory.

By the late 1930s, the debates on Keynes's theories and the knowledge gained from reflection on New Deal policies' compensatory spending established the outlines of fiscal policy as it is now known. Alvin E. Hansen of Harvard

University, among others, led the way in working out the theories of fiscal policy. Other economists at the University of Chicago fought a rearguard action, especially against the extravagances of Keynes's disciples who, like all disciples, went further than their master.

During World War II, economists continued to discuss fiscal policy and its uses in postwar stabilization. Economists now agree, as do leaders in political life, that there should be a fiscal policy for stability. As illustrated in the monetarist-Keynesian dispute, disagreement continues over the emphasis to be given fiscal and monetary policy and on their appropriate policy mix.

The propositions of income theory are briefly stated elsewhere in this book. Rules of abstract fiscal policy need not be restated here; they are contained in most texts on principles of economics. In any case, the real problems of concrete fiscal policy revolve about other matters.

How good a guide is abstract fiscal policy to concrete policy decisions that the U.S. Congress and parliaments of other countries have to make in a given year? Not good at all, is the monetarist answer. The gap between pure economic theory and usable policy recommendations exists everywhere and is by no means peculiar to fiscal policy. But this obvious reminder has to be given again, due to the over enthusiasm of some Keynesian economists for fiscal policy.

Abstract fiscal policy reaches its most exuberant expression in the writings of Keynesian economist Abba P. Lerner of Florida State University. He calls it "functional finance," and he would have the government simply adjust the total of all spending to eliminate both unemployment and inflation. Government expenditures, taxes, and printed money would be manipulated to force businesses and consumers to spend the right amounts.

Consider some fiscal policy proposals not of the abstract sort, but of the kind intended for concrete action by Congress. These proposals were at first called compensatory—the federal budget would compensate for the deficiency of aggregate demand after allowing for private consumption and investment. Federal expenditures were visualized as filling a large gap. It was not very long into the postwar era that economists began to see that the problem was one of stabilization rather than secular stagnation, that the task of successful economic forecasting was proving to be disappointingly hard, and that some reliance could be placed on built-in or automatic stabilizers.

One consequence was a search for a rule that, when followed, would cause the volume of federal expenditures and taxes to behave in such a way as to stabilize the economy. To put fiscal policy on an automatic rule would provide it with greater acceptance, especially among monetarists. A case in point is the 1947 proposal by the Committee on Economic Development (CED) for fiscal policy by rule, wherein the rule would be fixed tax rates, not to be modified except as a response to a major change in national policy.

Other examples of fixed policy rules include automatic flexibility and formula flexibility. The built-in stabilizer of the federal budget provides the automatic flexibility of tax revenues that fall and expenditures that rise when unemployment increases. The built-in stabilizers are not subject to recognition lags, let alone the administrative and operational ones. These automatic stabilizers cushion shocks and act as a first line of defense. They must be supplemented by additional measures of fiscal policy. Formula flexibility, on the other hand, is a modification of the rule concept. Under this concept, for instance, Congress would change the income tax laws so that rates (or exemptions or both) would move up and down in accordance with our appropriate economic index.

In 1949, economists from various shades of the political spectrum agreed that monetary policy in the United States and elsewhere was inoperative. It was not until 1951 (really 1953, at the end of the Korean War) in the United States, and later in other countries, that independent monetary policy began. Since that time, there has been little agreement on stability policy. Keynesians look to a strong fiscal policy with monetary policy as an adjunct. The monetarists place their reliance on a strong monetary policy accomplished by a rule-bound fiscal policy.

MONETARY AND FISCAL POLICY MIX

How should monetary and fiscal policy be mixed? Milton Friedman discussed this issue at some length during the height of the Korean War in 1951.[1] This was a period of military buildup in the United States, which pushed inflation into double digits.

Friedman argued that "monetary and fiscal measures are the only appropriate means of controlling inflation." He ruled out any recourse to wage-price controls. According to Friedman, monetary and fiscal measures are substitutes within a wide range. A large budget surplus would be consistent with no degree or, for that matter, any degree of inflation. In his view, a balanced budget would require tighter money to prevent inflation, and a budget deficit would require still tighter money. It is possible, according to Friedman, that budget deficits may get so large that they will simply overwhelm monetary policy. In fact, it may be impossible to design monetary policy that will prevent inflation. Consequently, there may not be a single best mix of monetary and fiscal policy and degree of inflation. According to Friedman, a good mix would be a roughly balanced budget (balanced over the business cycle) together with whatever associated monetary policy would prevent inflation. Moreover, no policy very far from this combination is likely to be appropriate.

As for high interest rates, in 1951 Friedman argued that while they curb investment expenditures, they also curb consumer expenditures, including spending on nondurable and durable goods. One reason, of course, is that high interest rates make saving more attractive. They also reduce the capital value of existing streams of wealth and thus reduce the ratio of wealth to income. In effect, high interest rates increase people's desire to add to their wealth.

High interest rates in 1951, as today, are not popular with many people for a variety of reasons. These reasons, however, are insufficient to overrule the requisite monetary policy to bring inflation under control. Thus it was that interest rates remained high in the early 1980s, at least in part because financial markets did not believe that inflation was under control. Indeed, some analysts argued at the time that financial markets believed that meant U.S. budget deficits slipped into Friedman's worst-case scenario and became so large that they ultimately overwhelmed monetary policy.

President Reagan's economic program was originally thought to be what the financial markets ordered. This assumption proved to be premature. Again, the debate was over interest rates and deficits. The key issue, according to some observers, was that long-term interest rates at the time embodied in them the expectation of deficits three or four years out. Financial markets feared that deficits would either stifle a recovery or rekindle inflation later. At the time, conventional wisdom on Wall Street was that uncertainty over the then record-breaking deficits in excess of the $100 billion Reagan proposed was a major reason—if not the only one—why interest rates were high. Lenders were demanding a high premium for their money because they did not know what economic conditions would prevail when they got paid back.

Moreover, there was a feeling widely shared in the U.S. financial community that the Reagan administration was not paying attention to their views. Indeed, the Reagan administration argument that neither the Federal Reserve nor the government can do anything about the persistence of high interest rates was less than reassuring to the financial community. This pessimistic view was, in fact, written into investors' expectations, and thus into high interest rates.

There is a considerable distance between the political and financial worlds. One explanation for the gulf of misunderstanding between the two worlds is mutual suspicion. Wall Street looks on the federal government as a "bloated monster loosed upon the land by vote-starved politicians." Washington, on the other hand, tends to think of Wall Street "as a tiny cell of conspirators secretly manipulating the markets of America to exploit Main Street."

In fact, deficits do matter. The U.S. economy can tolerate deficits less readily than other countries because the U.S. economy is a comparatively low-saving economy. For example, in recent years in Japan, personal savings, as a percentage of disposable personal income, was four times as large as in the United States. In the Federal Republic of Germany, it was about three times as large. Since the business sector is, in most countries, a net borrower, one must look at personal saving as the main source of surplus funds. In short, countries that save a lot (such as Germany, Japan, and Italy) experience less difficulty in financing a given level of deficit, expressed as a share of gross domestic product (GDP), than countries with lower rates of saving (such as the United States).

Although it is still a relatively low ratio to gross national product (GNP), the U.S. fiscal deficit accounts for a large share of available surplus funds and is of the same order of magnitude as total net outlays for new plant and equipment. When extra budgetary borrowing on behalf of other agencies is also taken into account, the current borrowing requirements of the federal government leave little of the surplus saving available for private sector borrowing. Unless the projected levels of fiscal deficits over the remainder of the 1990s can be reduced, only a very large expansion of private saving would prevent serious crowding out and upward pressure on interest rates.

Moreover, if a recent National Bureau of Economic Research study for the United States is correct (that there is a relatively fixed relationship between the total debt, both private and public, and GNP), the increase in public debt will imply a crowding out of private debt, with obvious implications for capital formation. In the United States, for example, total debt has averaged about 140 percent of GNP for several decades. In the 1960s, curiously, when the ratio of public debt to GNP in the United States was declining, the economy was growing at a lively pace. In the 1970s, when that ratio was either stationary or increasing, the rate of growth slowed down.

In essence, high fiscal deficits accompanied by tight monetary policies (as measured in terms of the rate of growth of the money supply) may not generate inflation, but nevertheless may raise interest rates and thus bring about a reduction in private productive activities. This reduction itself will magnify the size of the deficit through its built-in negative effects on revenues and positive effects on public expenditures. Germany, Japan, and the United States are important examples of countries that have in the past pursued tight monetary policies in the face of sizable fiscal deficits.

Suppose now that fiscal deficits are accompanied by an accommodating monetary policy. If the economy's productive capacities are fully utilized, the increase in aggregate demand will bring about increases in prices and wages. In the short urn, the increase in the money supply may bring about a decline in nominal interest rates as a result of the liquidity effect. Consumption will rise at the expense of saving as inflationary psychology prompts people to anticipate purchases. The demand for financial assets will fall, while that for real assets will rise, leading to a process of disintermediation in the capital market. Imports will expand, leading to a deterioration in the balance of payments. If exchange rates are fixed, there will be a loss in net foreign reserves that will tend to reduce the initial acceleration in the money supply growth. If exchange rates are flexible, the rate will depreciate, adding further to the domestic inflation rate. In short, high budgetary deficits accompanied by an accommodating monetary policy tend to aggravate inflation.

As an alternative to borrowing from the central bank or the private sector, governments can and do borrow abroad. For industrial countries where domestic capital markets are well integrated with those abroad, the process is direct if not always simple. Indeed, the evidence indicates that the practice of foreign borrowing to finance budget deficits has become prevalent since the 1970s, along with the rapid expansion of international financial markets, as both industrial and developing markets incurred significantly larger deficits. In fact, during the latter part of the 1970s, estimates place foreign deficit finance as about one sixth of industrial countries' budget deficits and one third of those of developing countries.

If borrowing by public enterprises could be accounted for, these percentages would no doubt be much higher.

Moreover, the recent pool of international saving provided by OPEC countries unable to absorb their saving internally has become smaller. Although perhaps it is still sufficient to accommodate requirements of the smaller developing countries, the pool is inadequate to meet U.S. needs and other industrial countries. If interest rates in the United States drift upward, the country will no doubt attract many of these funds and thus contribute to financing the U.S. deficit. This will tend to aggravate the capital-needs situation in developing countries and elsewhere; such developing countries will thereby face much stronger competition and higher interest rates. The implications are ominous for developing countries. Deficits of large countries do indeed have implications for the rest of the world.

Given the present and persistent size of fiscal deficits in many countries, authorities are severely restricted in their ability to use fiscal policy in a counter-cyclical fashion. To regain their freedom, countries are best advised to pursue policies that reduce budget deficits. This will enhance the chances that the negative effects of restrictive monetary policy will be removed and countries will be able to enjoy growth without inflation. Under these circumstances, persever-ance and political courage are required in dealing with the fiscal problem.

FISCAL POLICY AND CROWDING OUT

The monetarist view of fiscal policy is that pure fiscal expansion without monetary accommodation may influence national income in the short run. In the long run, however, such government expenditures will crowd out or replace some elements of private expenditure so that real income remains unchanged. If the reduction in private expenditure is identical in magnitude to the increase in government expenditure, the long-run fiscal multiplier is zero and crowding out is said to be complete. When the fiscal multiplier is greater than one, absence of crowding out is indicated. Crowding out is partial when the fiscal multiplier is between zero and one. In this instance, income rises by an amount less than the increase in government expenditure. Overcrowding is said to occur when the multiplier is negative. Private expenditures will fall by a greater magnitude than the rise in government expenditure.

The analysis of crowding out, moreover, can be done in real or nominal terms. I discuss elsewhere the technical and analytical issues involved in crowding out in both terms.[2] Suffice it here to note that one concept of crowding out does not imply the other; the distinction between them is important. Given expansionary fiscal operations on the part of government, various combinations of real and nominal crowding out are possible.

Presumably, the process also works in reverse. That is, reducing government expenditures may have the effect of "crowding in" private expenditures. This may have the effect, among others, of replacing unproductive government expenditures, thereby increasing the total output of goods and services in the economy. It is an implication that economists would accept.

To judge from studies made several years ago, the results indicate that crowding out does indeed occur.[3] It would seem that the question is no longer whether crowding out exists, but how much time it needs to occur. For instance, the Wharton Mark III model yielded a multiplier of -3 after thirty quarters, and the U.S. Department of Commerce model on the same period was -23. This is far in excess of a crowding out effect as defined by a steady-state government spending multiplier of near zero.

The performance of small monetarist models, such as that of the Federal Reserve Bank of St. Louis, suggests that crowding out occurs in a much shorter period of time than in the earlier Keynesian-type models. Moreover, crowding out occurs in nominal rather than in just real terms. The reported results in the St. Louis model indicate that government spending, as measured by high-employment expenditures, exercises a relatively strong influence on GNP, assuming a constant change in the money supply in the current quarter and the next quarter, but it is approximately offset within a year's time.

All of this, of course, does not mean that government spending does not matter. Indeed, it matters very much, especially if government expenditures accelerate or decelerate rapidly. The reduced form results of this St. Louis model are all the more interesting since they do not follow from a structural model that constrains the channels of transmission from fiscal actions to economic activity. This is consistent with the monetarist view that government expenditures cover a wide range of activities. They may substitute or complement private sector expenditures for consumption and investment. The diversity of these effects is apt to render limited any model that severely restricts the transmission channels of fiscal actions to income and/or interest rates. As such, the full impact of government expenditures on the private sector may be missed.

These and other simulation studies have served, and do indeed serve, as tools for policy makers, who use them along with other information to make public policy. The size and variability of monetary and fiscal policy multipliers that they yield leave much to be desired. Indeed, Michael Evans, a leading builder of large econometric models, agrees that econometric models built around Keynesian demand theories are seriously flawed, primarily because they ignore supply-side factors.[4] Moreover, failure to take into account recent data and changing economic structures (including legal and sociopolitical changes) limits the usefulness of these large econometric models for both simulation exercises and forecasting purposes. For instance, observers note that the parameters and multipliers of many models are typically based on people's past reactions to government policies. As such, their utility for policy-simulation purposes has limited value to policy makers, although these models may still be useful for forecasting purposes.

Forecasting, however, has its own shortcomings. No matter how sophisticated the econometric model used, it depends on the political and economic assumptions about government policies on which it rests. If these assumptions change, the models forecasts will likely be erroneous. Furthermore, since we cannot attach probability statements to economic forecasts, the utility of these models is limited. What we can. say is that if a forecaster could make the same forecast under the same conditions a very large number of times, he or she would be correct a certain percentage of the times—albeit within a certain range. This is not very useful, unfortunately, if we wish to forecast turning points in the GNP.[5]

This inability to forecast accurately has serious implications for stabilization policies, as we noted elsewhere. Together with variability of leads and lags in stabilization policies, erroneous forecasts have pushed some policy makers to reject short-run stabilization policies in favor of a policy of rules.

The finding of a strong empirical relationship between several measures of money and economic activity suggests that monetary policy can play a singularly important role in stabilization policy. Indeed, failure to recognize these relationships can have serious consequences on economic activity. These relationships to economic activity, moreover, appear more certain than fiscal actions.

Furthermore, the evidence provided in a number of Federal Reserve Board of St. Louis studies is consistent with other evidence, which suggests that the money stock is an important indicator of the total thrust of stabilization actions, both monetary and fiscal. In the first instance, changes in the money stock principally reflect discretionary actions of the Federal Reserve System as it uses open market operations, discount rate changes, and reserve requirements. Second, the money stock reflects the joint actions of the Treasury and Federal Reserve System in financing newly created government debt. These actions are based, in the final analysis, on decisions regarding the monetization of new debt by Federal Reserve actions, and Treasury decisions regarding changes in its balances at Reserve banks. Thus, changes in government spending financed by monetary expansion are reflected in changes in the monetary base and in the money supply.

As noted previously, many economists argue that the major influence of fiscal actions results only if expenditures are financed by monetary expansion. In the United States, the Federal Reserve does not buy securities from the government. Its open market operations, along with other actions, serve to provide funds in the markets in which both the government and private individuals borrow.

Moveover, it is not easy to reverse a stimulative stance in fiscal policy—a result in part of the institutional context in which fiscal tools are used. Some fiscal tools, such as automatic stabilizers, can be redirected quickly. These programs expand and contract more or less automatically in response to changes in the pace at which the economy is expanding. Such programs include unemployment compensation, welfare programs, leasing subsidies, and, in the United States, the progressive nature of the federal tax structure.

Some insight into how difficult it is to change the posture of fiscal policy quickly in either direction may be gained by considering that all new programs in the United States require congressional approval. This approval must be in a form that provides for the actions sought by the administration. Bills are sometimes changed in committee or on the floor of Congress in ways that significantly redirect their thrusts. Much the same is true in tax legislation. Political realities often intervene to make either raising or lowering taxes a long, drawn-out process. The political give-and-take may result in less than an optimal tax system.

Transfer payments, although they are outlays rather than taxes, are subject to the same forces that slow tax changes. Changes are likely to be a long time in coming, and temptation to embellish a proposed program is likely to be considerable. In fact, once recipients become accustomed to the payments, they and their political representatives will not be anxious to see them withdrawn when the need for stimulus passes. Discretionary changes in transfer payments thus tend to be one-way stabilization tools at best, for use when stimulus is needed.

According to some observers, fiscal policy in many countries, particularly in such critical years as the 1960s and 1970s, has become a major destabilizing force.[6] Indeed, many of the transfer programs and other benefits were introduced when their cost was low and their future fiscal consequences were ignored. In other cases, highly optimistic forecasts about important variables, such as growth, unemployment, and inflation, were made at the time the programs were introduced or expanded, mainly during the 1960s and early 1970s. Changed circumstances since those years have made it very difficult for many countries to keep their commitments and still pursue a sound fiscal policy.

INFLATION TAX

Inflation is a method for raising revenue by a special kind of tax. This is a tax on the real money holdings, or, in the technical jargon of the economist, on the real cash balances of individuals.

When a government is either too weak or is unwilling on grounds of political expediency to enact adequate tax programs and to administer them effectively, it resorts to inflation as a method of raising revenue. This tax is often appealing because it does not require detailed legislation and can be administered simply. All that is required is to spend the newly created money. The resulting inflation automatically imposes a tax on the real money holdings or cash balances of individuals. The tax rate is the rate of depreciation in the real value of money, which is equal to the rate of rise in prices. The revenue (in real terms) in the product of this base and the rate. The money-issuing authorities collect all the revenue. When prices rise in greater proportion than the quantity of money (demand deposits, time deposits, and currency in public bonds)—that is, when the real value of cash balances declines—part of the revenue goes to reduce the real value of the outstanding money supply. At the same time, inflation also reduces the real value of the principal and interest charges of debt fixed in money or nominal terms. Thus total revenue for a period of time is the sum of two factors: (1) the real value of new money issued per period of time; and (2) the reduction in outstanding monetary liabilities, equal to the decline per period of time in the real value of cash balances. It should be noted, however, that the money-issuing authorities do not set the tax directly. They set the rate at which they increase the money supply, and this rate is effected through the willingness of individuals to hold and not spend the additional money supply.

Institutions other than the government have money-issuing powers. Insofar as these institutions exercise these powers, they share in some of the revenue from tax, even though the initiating factor is government creation of money. However, in past inflations, these other institutions for the most part largely dissipated the revenue from their share of the tax. Banks, for example, largely dissipated their share by making loans at minimal rates of interest that did not take full account of the subsequent rise in prices. Thus the real rate of interest received was, on the average, below the real return that could be obtained on capital. The revenue dissipated went to the borrowers.

The revenue received by the government consequently depends on the tax base, the tax rate, and the fraction of the revenue that goes either to institutions such as banks or to their borrowers. However, a higher tax rate will not yield a proportionately higher revenue because the tax base, or the level of real cash balances, will decline in response to a higher rate. As an increasing number of people begin to believe in the inevitability of inflation, their money holdings will ultimately decline more than in proportion to the rise in tax rate, so that a higher rate will yield less revenue. It is at this point that inflation enters into a transition between "creeping" and "galloping" varieties.

The productivity of taxation through inflation has been examined by Phillip Cagan. In his study of severe hyperinflation (galloping inflation), Cagan found that the actual share of national income procured for different governments that used inflation as a means of taxation was 3 to about 15 percent, except for Imperial Russia, which had an unusually low percentage of 0.5.[7] In almost all cases, the revenue collected by the inflationary tax was lower on average than could have been collected by other means of taxation, given that the respective countries had a stable growth in the money supply.

The recent rediscovery of issuing inflation-proof government debt promised savers that they will have a safe haven for their savings. The United States Treasury appears ready to issue index-linked debt (i.e., bonds whose interest payments and principal are tied to inflation).[8] In America, the practice was already known in 1780, when Massachusetts issued bonds that promised that payments of both interest and principal would not be fixed in money terms, but would depend on the price of "five bushels of corn, sixty-eight pounds and four-seventh parts of a pound of bee, ten pounds of sheep's wool and sixteen pounds of sole leather."[9] The reason for such a venture was that inflation was high and hard to predict, given that there was a war, which made lenders wary of ordinary bonds.

A BALANCED BUDGET AMENDMENT?

Attempts to address the issue of federal deficits that stem from unbalanced budgets—budgets that spend more than they take in through taxation—is a recurring theme in American politics, especially since World War II. The questions asked are familiar enough: Should the federal budget be balanced by law, as many state and local budgets are? Should the United States adopt a constitutional amendment requiring a balanced federal budget?

Just such questions were asked in 1982 when President Reagan pushed forward to Congress proposals for a balanced budget amendment to the Constitution. Although the balanced budget proposal did not pass Congress, it did generate considerable support. In fact, support for the proposal makes it an ongoing issue before Congress and elsewhere. Does the proposal for a balanced budget amendment make any sense?

Clearly, the continuing federal budget deficits since the 1960s have done little to reduce unemployment and may, in fact, have complicated the problem of economic stability and growth of the American economy. Proponents of a constitutional amendment argue that balanced budgets would serve to stabilize the economy by removing the instability of government action.

Such an amendment, moreover, would serve to cut federal programs, many of which are expensive and wasteful. Proponents note that spending is harder to cut than many people imagine. Attempts to cut spending in the early 1980s simply raised deficits, in good part because of the deep recession in the 1980s. Income transfers automatically increased to help the unemployed, who paid less tax because they earned less wages and income.

Apparently, runaway government spending cannot be controlled through tax cuts. The proponents thus turn to a constitutional amendment as the only serious legal route to force expenditures down to the level of tax receipts. The political motives behind the balanced budget amendment are not always clear. Some people see it as a way to reduce social programs, others as a means to reduce defense expenditures, and so on. Still others favor a budget amendment rather than a constitutional correction with unforeseen consequences, including greater government restrictions of one kind or another on individual rights.

The fact is that as simple as a balanced budget amendment looks (i.e., expenditures = revenues), the devil is in the details. Would the government resort to expansion via creiture expenditures, as it did in the 1980s and as it did through tax expenditures in the 1970s? Or would the government's influence on allocation and distribution through taxing spending, transfers, tax expenditures, and so forth be reduced in unpredictable and unexpected ways?

Debt is a major government revenue source. Government borrowing, and tax collection, goes by many names. It includes deficits, deficit spending, deficit finance, taxes (including taxes through inflation) and bond financing. The impact on the economy of such government activities are many and diverse. Attempts to constrain such activities through a balanced budget amendment are laudable, but too many people will find that task no easy chore. It simply is not easy to amend the American constitution; three fourths of the states must ratify an amendment once it gets through Congress.

NOTES

1. See, for example, Milton Friedman, ed., *Essays in Positive Economics* (Chicago: University of Chicago Press, 1953). See also H. Stein, *Fiscal Revolution in America* (Chicago: University of Chicago Press, 1969).

2. See George Macesich, *Monetarism: Theory and Policy* (Westport, CT: Praeger, 1983), pp. 168–183.

3. For example, see Gary Fromm and Lawrence R. Klein, "A Comparison of Eleven Econometric Models of the United States," *American Economic Review* (May 1973), pp. 385–393; Lawrence R. Klein, "Commentary on the State of the Monetarist Debate," *Review*, Federal Reserve Bank of St. Louis (September 1973), pp. 9–12; K. M. Carlson, "Monetary and Fiscal Actions in Macroeconomic Models," *Review*, Federal Reserve Bank of St. Louis (January 1974), pp. 8–18; R. W. Hafer, "The Role of Fiscal Policy in the St. Louis Equation," *Review*, Federal Reserve Bank of St. Louis (January 1982), pp. 17–22.

4. Michael Evans, "Bankruptcy of Keynesian Econometric Models," *Challenge* (January/February 1980), pp. 13–19.

5. See, for instance, Victor Arnowitz, "On the Accuracy and Properties of Recent Macroeconomic Forecasts," *American Economic Review* (May 1976), pp. 313–319.

6. See, for instance, J. de Larosier, "Coexistence of Fiscal Deficits: High Tax Burdens in Consequence of Pressures for Public Spending," *IMF Survey*, March 22, 1982, p. 82.

7. These occurred in Austria, October 1921 to August 1922; in Germany, August 1922 to July 1923; in Greece, November 1943 to August 1944; in Hungary, March 1923 to February 1924 and again in August 1945 to February 1946; in Poland, January 1923 to November 1923; and in Imperial Russia, December 1921 to January 1924. Phillip Cagan, "The Monetary Dynamics of Hyper Inflation," in Milton Friedman, ed., *Studies in the Quantity Theory of Money* (Chicago: University of Chicago Press, 1956), pp. 25–117. See also Milton Friedman, "Government Revenue from Inflation," *Journal of Political Economy* (July/August 1971), especially pp. 852–854.

8. See "Of Beef, Bushes, and Bonds," *The Economist*, May 25, 1996, p. 84.

9. Ibid., p. 84.

Chapter 8

Government Regulation and Control of Business

THE ISSUE OF COMPETITIVENESS

The United States in the mid-1990s led the world in competitiveness, followed by Asia powerbases Singapore, Hong Kong, and Japan. Switzerland and Germany registered ninth and tenth places, while Great Britain and France came in nineteenth and twentieth places, respectively. Unfortunately, Russia came in last. These rankings are reported by the International Institute for Management Development. They are based on measures of competitiveness that attempt to gauge mechanisms that help create wealth in a nation.

The Institute's estimates use approximately 230 criteria covering economic strength, technology, technical services, international trade, government policies, management, infrastructure, and educational skills. The United States is a standout in the areas of economic strength, new technology, and financial services and places second in international trade. America's weakness apparently lies in people skills (education and training); it placed as fifteenth among forty-six countries.

The Institute attributes the high ranking given the United States to bold economic reforms, deregulation and privatization and renewed leadership in new technology. At the same time, however, these results may well imply that the income of certain employees was frozen while productivity grew rapidly.

Asian countries continued to excel in the mid-1990s. This was reflected in their ranking by strength of their domestic economies: China, second; Singapore, third; Korea, fourth; Japan, fifth; Malaysia, seventh; and Hong Kong, eighth. China rose from thirty-first in 1995 to twenty-sixth in 1996, while Taiwan slipped from fourteenth to eighteenth. Japan continued to have problems. It scored second in management and technology but dropped to twenty-first place for government policies.

Another study on the competitiveness issue undertaken by Jeffrey Sachs, director of the Harvard Institute for International Development, for the Swiss-based World Economic Forum presents somewhat different evaluation criteria.[1] Sachs defines competitiveness as the ability of a nation's economy to make rapid and sustained gains in living standards. Such a definition is useful in that it avoids the zero-sum-game aspect of competitiveness, in which one country's success comes at the expense of other countries. He puts more weight on objective measures such as average tariffs, savings as a percentage of GDP and numbers of telephone lines per capita. Other factors in the index include findings from surveys of international business executives on their feel for such factors as security of property rights and the international experience of senior management.

Based on Sachs's criteria, Singapore is ranked first, with Hong Kong, New Zealand, the United States, Luxembourg, and Switzerland following. Russia is last, with Brazil, Venezuela, Hungary, and India little ahead of Russia. Apart from the United States and New Zealand, the top-ranked countries have small and very open economies that specialize in providing trade and financial services to the world.

Another group rated by Sachs are the so-called Anglo-Saxon economies such as New Zealand (ranked third), the United States (fourth), Canada (eighth), Australia (twelfth) and Britain (fifteenth). These countries do far better due to their flexibility and lack of inclination to solve every problem through government intervention.

Although they have a high rank, many of the Asian countries slipped from their past performance: Taiwan (ninth) is followed by Malaysia (tenth), Thailand (fourteenth) and South Korea (twentieth). Many affluent economies do relatively poorly: Japan (thirteenth), the Netherlands (seventeenth), Germany (twenty-second) and France (twenty-third) are bunched in the middle. The report cites that their relatively low ranking reflects in part the fiscal, financial, and employment problems confronting the social welfare countries of Europe.

The report rests on the theoretical base that long-term growth largely turns on the openness to trade, commitment to free markets, investment in technology and human skills, rule of law, and stability. On this evaluation, some economies that have done relatively well in recent years will either have to reevaluate their efforts and policies or slip much lower in rank. In particular such countries as China (thirty-sixth), Indonesia (thirtieth) the Czech Republic (thirty-fifth) and Italy (forty-first) would do well to examine their policies. The index is intended to predict future capacity for growth and rest on past performance.

In any case, most economists agree that growth is indeed driven by such factors as the rule of law, stability, open markets, high savings, and human capital. It may be nonsense that countries compete in the same way as companies; when two companies compete, one's gain is the other's loss. When two countries compete through trade, they both win.

The rush to downsize many companies and thus to remain competitive has gained worldwide recognition. Governments have set up committees to examine how to sharpen their country's economic performance. It is important for these committees and their members to understand that a country's future prosperity depends on its growth in productivity, which government policies can indeed influence. Countries do compete in the sense that they choose policies to promote higher living standards for their citizens.

LAW AND ECONOMIC POLICY

If we wish to understand American economic policy, at least a nodding acquaintance is required with the Constitution as a living document. The American Constitution both guides and limits the federal and state governments in their exercise of controls over economic policy Most people are well aware of the importance of legal questions and how pervasive they are in the operation of economic controls, environmental requirements, and safety laws. Thousands of major and minor legal issues are decided each year by the legal staffs of federal and state agencies.

In the United States, the Constitution establishes the legal form as well as the legal boundaries of economic policy. Moreover, the Constitution founded the separation of powers of government as well as the federal system, both of which have singularly important consequences for American economic policy.[2] Government can be taken to mean something in the abstract as an ideal or something that is perceived as maximizing social welfare or as a process of complex interacting groups or as a real entity consisting of a large group of federal and state legislatures, courts, and representative departments and agencies. Government as a real entity is in fact the reality with which business and other actors learn to deal.[3] It is in this sense that the relation between government and business is discussed.

The American Constitution is embedded in a body of laws, even though it is in fact the supreme law of the country. All other laws must conform to the Constitution. Nonetheless, common law and the law of equity do provide a foundation given that such laws are older than the Constitution.

The importance of Anglo-American tradition of common law is that it recognizes the social advantages of competition. A general principle of common law is that if businesspeople enter into contracts that contain restraints of trade, such contracts cannot be legally enforced. Another point of importance to modern economic policies is the concept of common calling. In effect, a seller has the right to refuse to sell his or her wares to any buyer for whatever reason. Common law did take into account certain exceptions, which included possessors of local monopoly positions. Upon them the common law imposed the duty of serving all consumers at reasonable rates.

It is important to underscore that common law has no preventive feature.[4] It operates from case to case, from one individual lawsuit to another. This means, for instance, that in some economic policies that have the specific aim of preventing damage in protection of consumers and producers, the ancient maxim of let the buyer beware is set aside. The reason for the exception is that the law is slow in dealing with such issues. Special protective legislation speeds the legal process and so makes protection active rather than passive.

Even though common law does not contain a preventive measure, the law of equity does provide for rapid remedial action. Thus a court, whether federal or state, can sit in equity whereby a speedy and equitable solution is achieved to problems that cannot be handled by ordinary processes of law. For instance, a court sitting in equity may issue an injunction to prevent irreparable damage to one party (A) as a consequence of action by another party (B). Violation of the injunction is taken to be in contempt of court and so punished. In fact, the injunction instrument has been largely aimed at labor disputes to stop violence, picketing, and boycotts. The growing political power of labor unions and other sympathetic groups has modified the exercise of the injunction instrument by both federal and state courts.

The separation of powers of government in the American Constitution into the legislature, the executive, and judicial has not made easy the formation and coordination of economic policies. As a result, there is often considerable tension and at times conflict between the executive and legislative branches over policies, including economic policy.

The Constitution allocates to Congress such express powers as control over the monetary system, interstate commerce, and foreign trade. To these powers can be added the so-called implied powers, which give Congress added authority. As for the states, their police powers permit them to legislate for the health and welfare of their citizens and residents. Judicial review has served as a constraint to the intentions of Congress and state legislatures. In fact, the courts have managed to hold federal and state economic controls within limits. Increasingly, the Constitution is regarded as the protector of not only the business interests but those of labor as well. Much of the legal system has come about through legislation and positions of the Supreme Court, especially since the 1930s.

Moreover, national federal economic policy has come to dominate the American economic scene even though states increasingly are involved in economic regulation. Many industries are regulated by both federal and state agencies. Federal and state relations have grown piecemeal and so on many points are inconsistent or in conflict with one another. On some broad issues and areas, substantial agreement does exist.

The administrative commission tends to be the principal legal arrangement for the regulation of individual industries in the United States.[5] Earlier direct control of industry by legislatures was abandoned in favor of the commission method.

The growing importance of the scholarly movement known as law and economics is viewed by many observers as providing for its insights into the issues cast up by the legal system and market.[6] This movement analyzes legal problems in terms of the costs and benefits faced by rational, self-interested individuals. Alternative solutions are evaluated by asking which set of incentives and disincentives will promote the most efficient use of resources involved.

Legal scholars turn to economics, which has paradigms that provide an analytic framework useful for the examination of many legal issues. These paradigms, and economic theory in general, are useful. Particularly useful to legal scholars and lawyers is the concept of self-interest in economic theory. For the legal profession, the concept of self-interest and its relation to an efficient allocation of resources helps to simplify a complex world created in part by the diversity of values among people.

There are, however, some obvious limitations to a blanket application of economics to law. For one, the economist's concept of a rational person is one who seeks to maximize his or her own self-interest. His or her concern for the well-being of others is limited. The self-centered drive produces outcomes in which private and social costs diverge. As a consequence, outcomes can conflict with society's general interest. Private maximization of profit can be inconsistent with the attainment of society's aims and objectives.

The other limitation in the lawyer's concept of a reasonable person is distinct from the economist's rational person. According to traditional tort literature, the reasonable person will ordinarily balance in a reasonable, prudent manner. He or she will act with fair regard for the welfare of others. Thus, negligent conduct that departs from the standard of the reasonable man is deviant and serves to justify the imposition of liability rules on tortfeasars. In effect, it is the difference between the incrementalism of the economist's rational person and the court's binary aspect of the lawyer's person that which finds the defendant either liable or not liable.

Due to rapid industrialization and urbanization, which have greatly increased the interdependence of people, tort law is a growing body of law. The increased complexities of modern society serve to underscore this interdependence. The desire to protect the common person and society from the destruction of the environment is an example.

Along with tort law, environmental law has grown out of society's concern with defining, enforcing, and allocating environmental property rights and entitlements. Again because of the economic and legal complexities in dealing with environmental issues, the courts and legislatures have been called on to interfere. On this score cost-benefit analysis is a useful analytical device. Although courts and legislatures have been slow in making use of empirical cost-benefit analyses, they do appear to have made use of this analytical technique in many instances.

Economics and law are used by legislatures to deal with threats to the environment by levying a variety of taxes and fees. In other instances they have provided subsidies to induce environmentally safer practices. At the same time, legislatures have encouraged firms and households to adopt such practices through appropriate incentives.

MAINTAINING AND PROMOTING COMPETITION

Given the private nature of the American economy, it must be competitive. A key objective of the country's economic policy is to maintain and create competition. The policy poses problems due to the nature of the American economy and to serious differences of opinion regarding how such a policy is to be formulated and executed.

It is useful to have a clear conception of what competition is. Broadly, competition is a set of relations among producers and consumers, a discipline compelling producers to act in certain ways, a discipline forcing them into patterns of behavior compatible with procedure and the efficient use of resources. As such, competition can take many forms.

Before the 1930s, competition as such posed no particular problem of definition. It was competition and its opposite was monopoly. On occasion, special forces of competition such as oligopoly were also discussed, particularly in economic literature. Matters changed in 1933 with the publication of the economic works of the American economist Edward H. Chamberlain and the English economist Joan Robinson.[7] With the publication of the Chamberlain and Robinson studies, competition as a single concept was broken down into several. One consequence of such a breakdown is disagreement of both theory and policy.

In any case, most observers agree that for policy the relevant concept is workable competition. Its essential elements are that sellers of closely similar products are numerous enough that no single seller and/or group can dominate a market and there is freedom of entry and exit from the industry. Given these conditions and with active competition among sellers, buyers have a good assortment of alternative products or services. Some observers emphasize market structure. Other observers emphasize standards of performance of an industry or effectiveness of the competition prevailing in it. It is useful to consider both sets of criteria in judging competition in an industry.

In the case of monopoly, it is difficult to assign a usefully precise statement of degrees of monopoly power either for theoretical or policy purposes. Theoretically, monopoly is some degree of control over price. For policy as well as for legal purposes, monopoly power has several dimensions, including (besides price control) control over entry and over the actions of competition.

In judging the actual extent of competition in the American economy, economists and other observers disagree. Some argue that competition in America has been declining for several decades.[8] Other observers produce studies that there has been no marked tendency for competition to decline since the turn of the century.[9] The early studies in declining competition may have been influenced by the many definitions of competition after 1933 as discussed by Watson.[10] Indeed, the tendency after 1933 was a much freer and loose application of the term *monopoly* to business firms in the United States. The existing empirical estimates of competition in the American economy do not appear to support the thesis that it is declining. In fact, given the nature of local markets in the United States, there was probably as much if not more opportunity for decreased competition in the nineteenth and early twentieth centuries as there is now.

In any event, the preservation and promotion of competition is an ongoing task for public policy. There is little doubt that the temptation exists for individuals and groups to break with the economic descriptive provided by competition. The control of prices and production and so departure from competition takes many forms. Explicit agreement among the parties to compromise competition is not always necessary. Moreover, the size of some business firms may enable them to cut down or eliminate competition.

Large businesses may be a problem due to their ability to achieve substantial economies of operation. Again, the existing empirical evidence does not indicate a clear superiority of large corporations. It is possible to argue on both sides of the issue for and against big business. The 1980s and 1990s suggested that a number of the large American firms were determined to reduce their size.

It is important to keep in mind that competition serves consumer interests. Simply stated, consumer interest is not organized and depends on competition. Business, labor, and other organized groups are in position to compromise competition among their own members. Organized interest groups can and do reduce the degree of competitiveness of the economy as a whole. Organized interest groups may also work for competition, as when small businesspeople push for tighter controls on big businesses.

One problem presented by attempts in a free society to preserve and promote competition is the preservation of the right of freedom of association. After all, freedom includes everyone's right to form and join organizations with lawful purposes. Nevertheless, such organizations may induce patterns of behavior that may be incompatible with effective competition.

The American economy's experience with labor unions and collective bargaining has on occasion pushed on the objection of preserving competition. In their collective bargaining activities, unions do exert varying degrees of monopoly power. Perhaps for this reason, unions are very sensitive to the use of the term *monopoly* to describe their activities. At the same time, their opponents have no such reservation in attributing monopoly power to unions. At times, unions have aligned themselves with business groups to suppress competition. Again, at issue is the problem of the right of freedom of association as well the problem of proper and improper exercise of union power.

In effect, no single powerful lobby group supports competition. Various interest groups serve to weaken a policy preserving and promoting competition. Economic literature provides abundant evidence that competition is in the general or public interest. The advantages of competition are mostly in the long run, even though some are apparent from day to day. Present policy does seek to prevent restrictions on competition and so contributes to the broadly competitive character of the American economy.

There never has been a systematic, comprehensive effort to make the American economy more competitive.[11] Antitrust policy has operated in bits and pieces, in fits and starts. No attempt has been made to find those areas in which competition is weakest. Such enforcement as has taken place has come almost entirely from the investigation of complaints. Since the late 1930s, both the prosecution of violations of the antitrust laws and court interpretations of these laws have developed in the direction of a stronger policy. It is, however, strong only in comparison. The concentration of economic power in the American economy remains much as it has for many years. Present policy limits the ways by which big corporations can grow bigger. It also seeks to prevent restrictions on competitive action.

Consider now the tools and measures available to the government to preserve and promote competition in the American economy. Economists have worked with lawyers in designing various measures to cope with issues of competition and specifically with the problems of monopoly, antitrust, and price fixing. The complexities flowing from differences in philosophies, economic analyses, and interpretations of fact create considerable tensions in dealing with these problems.

It is not surprising that there is widespread dissatisfaction with antitrust policy in the United States. Anti-trust policy was the product of early American experience even before the passage at the turn of the century of the Sherman and Clayton Acts. These experiences have been woven into the interpretation by the courts. The courts have not always given clear signals in their rendering decisions. On more than one occasion since 1890, Congress has been sufficiently aroused about antitrust policy to hold long and detailed investigations.

Given the political environment when the Sherman Act was adopted in 1890, it is to be expected that strong views at first suppressed would eventually surface. The Sherman Act was passed with little debate and without a clash of interests. Politicians from all parties wanted to register their disapproval of trusts by approving antitrust measures. By 1890, all political parties had to have anti-monopoly planks in their platforms.

In any case, political agitation continued during the first decade of the twentieth century, in good part due to the dissatisfaction with the Sherman Act. The language of the Act gave considerable latitude to the courts, and the rule of reason made enforcement difficult owing to the necessity of the government's need to prove unreasonableness.

With the subsequent adoption of the Clayton and Federal Trade Commission Acts of 1914, the legal care of the antitrust policy was in place. As a result, two principal changes in economy policy were made. The Clayton Act was to specify the monopolistic practices to be prohibited. The Federal Trade Commission (FTC) was expected to be the economic policy arm of the government. As matters developed, however, the FTC declined in importance. Various court decisions weakened the laws it was enforcing, it lost support, and eventually even the quality of its bureaucracy declined.

Antitrust policy had only moderate success in curbing the monopoly power of large business enterprises. The policy success that was achieved was probably due more to its deterrent effects. On the issues of antimerger policy, the Clayton Act was powerless until 1950, when it was amended to prohibit the acquisition of assets. Again, success can probably be attributed to the deterrent effects of the major successful prosecutions of big business in the post-World War II period. Price-fixing violations have been easier to prosecute due to the lack of reasonableness as a defense by those parties so charged.

Action against exclusion and price discrimination is also undertaken in antitrust policy. The idea is to draw a line between those business practices that conflict with and those that are consistent with the requirement of competition. The line is anything but precise.

Trade associations can limit competition through various techniques that can be effective, such as direct agreements on prices and production. It is difficult for the enforcing agency to prove that there is an intention to limit price competition and that the trade association in question has enough market power to be successful. Thus it is not surprising that not many suits have been brought against trade associations, and of those charged, some have been dismissed for lack of evidence.

Exclusive dealerships and tying clauses are another form of restriction on competition, but again it is very difficult to prove that such restrictions are in practice. Exclusive arrangements can come under the Sherman Act prohibition of contracts in unreasonable restraint of trade. These practices, moreover, could also be unfair methods of competition under Section 5 of the Federal Trade Commission Act, and they could violate Section 3 of the Clayton Act, which prohibits tying contracts that could "substantially" lessen competition.[12]

Price discrimination, the selling of the same commodity or service at different prices during a given period of time, is an ongoing practice in many parts of the American economy. As such, the practice has been a problem in economic policy. It takes many forms, from the accepted to unaccepted, from the legal to the illegal. The Clayton Act of 1914 prohibits price discrimination if and only if it limits competition. The difficulty of executing this policy prompted the Robinson-Patman Act of 1936, which is viewed as an amendment to the Clayton Act, presumably to clarify the policy on price discrimination. The confusion and controversy that the issue of price discrimination provokes are likely to continue.

Other policies carried out by the government are supplementary to its antitrust efforts. Their objectives are similar: mainly to preserve and promote competition. The American patent system grants inventors monopolies on their inventions, which appears contrary to objective of promoting competition. In fact, American patent policy is firmly lodged in the Constitution, which vests Congress with the power to promote and encourage inventors with patents. As such, the patent policy is much older than the express policy to preserve and promote competition. Indeed, American patent laws can be traced back three hundred years to British law.

In antitrust law and patent law, two major policies conflict. Economists who support a strong antimonopoly policy suggest reforms that preserve incentives for inventors and so continued technological advance while at the same time encouraging competition. One such policy recommendation is to compel patent owners to allow the use of their property in return for reasonable royalties. The Patent Act of 1952, which overhauled and codified patent, laws is essentially a conservative piece of legislation. It is thus unlikely that significant reform will occur. The interests that wish to keep the status quo are simply too strong.

The Federal Trade Commission does attempts to keep unfair methods of competition to a minimum. False advertising continues to be a problem, particularly in such products as foods, drugs, and cosmetics. Pure food and drug legislation is an attempt to protect consumers. Other measures and policies that supplement antitrust efforts include provision of information, supervision of organized markets, and regulation of the issue of new securities.

State governments have tended to weaken competition in areas not covered by antitrust laws. The states have their own antitrust laws, though few of them enforce these laws with any vigor. Moreover, state governments also tend to protect industries within their own borders and thus restrict competition even more.

If competition is to be preserved and promoted, it is important that the federal and state governments work toward this common end. Unfortunately, this is not the case. States tend to undermine federal efforts in many important instances. The federal government is not always alone in the pursuit of competition, in good part because it fails to coordinate its other economic policies with competition.

The Sherman Act, Clayton Act, and other measures apply only to interstate commerce. Although the concept of commerce has been expanded since 1937, a good deal of intrastate commerce is still excluded and not subject to federal laws. As we note, state governments are not particularly enthusiastic in promoting and preserving competition, nor in maintaining freedom of entry, nor in preventing unfair competition. In fact, many of their policies run counter to the objective of federal antitrust laws. One reason, perhaps, is that state legislatures more than Congress tend to be dominated by organized business and labor groups, so the distribution of political power in the states serves to undermine such polices as antitrust.[13]

State barriers to competition such as general preference laws are but a case in point.[14] Employment with the state or on state contracts goes to residents of the state; purchases by the state government must be from, or preference must be given to, businesses located within the state; and, in general, all printing for the state government must be done within the state. These general preference laws seemingly underscore that public policy pursues goals other than the maintenance and promotion of competition.

More than one observer has called attention to federal fiscal policy as a source for undermining competition. Indeed, some argue that the effect of the immediate post–World War II federal fiscal policy was to undermine much of the work of previous antitrust enforcement.[15] The point is that the structure of fiscal policy was warped by the pressure from powerful organized interest groups, which in effect succeeded in causing the instruments of fiscal policy to undermine competition and so strengthened and promoted monopoly. Thus tax concessions granted to corporations during the period of the Korean War did much to strengthen the positions of large corporations.[16] A company was granted what amounted to a temporary reduction in corporate income taxes when it built a plant judged to be for national defense. To the extent that it contributed to further concentration in industry, such tax measures worked to undermine competition.

There is also a tendency for the effects of federal taxes on the growth of small firms to be more severe than on the growth of their large corporate competitors. Taxes may even pressure companies to sell out or merge with others. The net effect serves to undermine competition. In short, federal tax policy conflicts at some point with the objectives of the country's antitrust laws.

NOTES

1. See Peter Passell, "Economic Scene," *The New York Times*, Thursday, June 6, 1996, p. C2; "The C-Word Strikes Back," *The Economist* (June 1, 1996), 339:7968, p. 76.

2. See Donald S. Watson, *Economic Policy* (Boston: Houghton Mifflin, 1960).

3. See, for instance, the discussion in Anthony Downs, *An Economic Theory of Democracy* (New York: Harper, 1957).

4. Watson, *Economic Policy*, p. 174.

5. See Marver H. Bernstein, *Regulating Business by Independent Commission* (Princeton, NJ: Princeton University Press, 1955).

6. See Richard A. Posner, *Overcoming Law* (Cambridge: Harvard University Press, 1994); and Werner Z. Hirsch, *Law and Economics* (New York: Academic Press, 1979).

7. Edward H. Chamberlain, *The Theory of Monopolistic Competition* (Cambridge: Harvard University Press, 1933); Joan Robinson, *The Economics of Imperfect Competition* (London: Macmillan, 1933). For a discussion of the forms and problems of definition, see Watson, *Economic Policy,* pp. 200–227.

8. See Arthur Robert Burns, *The Decline of Competition* (New York: McGraw-Hill, 1936).

9. See George J. Stigler, "Competition in the United States," *Five Lectures in Economic Problems* (New York: Macmillan, 1950), pp. 46–65; G. Warren Nutter, *The Extent of Enterprise Monopoly in the United States, 1899–1939* (Chicago: University of Chicago Press, 1951); Harvey J. Levin (ed.), *Business Organization and Public Policy* (New York: Rinehart, 1958). See, for instance, Walter Adams and Horace M. Gray, *Monopoly in America: The Government as Promoter* (New York: Macmillian, 1955), p. 74.

10. Watson, *Economic Policy*, p. 216.

11. Ibid., p. 250.

12. For a discussion of exclusive dealerships and tying clauses see Irwin M. Stelzer, *Selected Antitrust Cases* (Homewood, IL: Irwin, 1955), Chapter 6; Joel B. Dirlam and Alfred E. Kahn, *Fair Competition* (Ithaca, NY: Cornell University Press, 1954), Chapters 4 and 6; Watson, *Economic Policy*, Chapter 12.

13. See Vernon A. Mund, *Government and Business* (New York: Harper, 1955), Chapter 20.

14. See Watson, *Economic Policy*, p. 321.

15. See, for instance, Walter Adams and Horace M. Gray, *Monopoly in America: The Government as Promoter* (New York: Macmillan, 1955), p. 74.

16. Ibid., p. 74.

Chapter 9

Policy Toward Labor and Its Organizations

AN ATTITUDE CHANGE

The importance of promoting and preserving competition in the American economy is a singularly important public policy goal. On most measures of performance, the American economy scores well. Its weakness lies in such areas as training, among others, that tend to diminish the quality of important segments of the American labor force.

Our discussion of business corporations underscored the impact of public policy on their activities. In the United States, the federal and state governments exhibit long-standing support and encouragement of business through such measures as incorporation laws, tax advantages, and many others. It is only since the 1930s, however, that the federal government has favored the formation of labor unions. To the extent that such public policy encourages or permits large labor organizations, it collides with public policy promoting competition.

The attitude of the federal government toward labor and its organization of labor unions is enmeshed with policies that aim at reducing inequalities of income. Considerable controversy exists on the issue of if in fact labor and its unions have sufficient market power to raise the incomes of their members. Whatever the evidence, a strong presumption exists that unions do have such power. It was based on such beliefs, shared by many people, that a strong push was made in the 1930s to promote unions and collective bargaining as a means for raising wages. This position was further supported by people who wished to redress the political and social power of business organizations by supporting the growth and power of labor and its organization.

It is obvious that American economic policy before the 1930s was generally opposed to labor organizations. A quick review of the country's experience underscores that federal and state statutes and court decisions were either neutral or made it very difficult to form and operate labor organizations. It is true that as early as the mid-ninteenth century, the United States did recognize the right of a group of wage earners to agree to go on strike. It is also true that a considerable gap existed between the right to strike and the formation and promotion of unions. Many changes in legal doctrine had to take place before unions in the United States were considered and accepted as legitimate organizations for labor. In fact, it was not until the Norris-LaGuardia Act of 1932 that the federal government's attitude toward labor dispute became, at best, neutral.

Although the Clayton Act was an attempt to remove the antitrust handicap from unions, it was not until the Wagner Act of 1935 that great changes occurred, when employers were obligated to enter into collective bargaining positions with unions. The National Labor Relations Board certifies unions as collective bargaining agents and prevents employers from interfering with the functioning of unions. A reaction to the Wagner Act resulted in the passage of the Taft-Hartley Act of 1947, which imposed obligations on unions. Nevertheless, a policy that now encourages unions is in place in the United States.

For all practical purposes, public policy is now essentially silent on union market power, which is in contrast to the antitrust policy of limiting the power of business organizations. No federal policy as such exists that restricts the size and scope of union activity. Indeed, there is little agreement on whether federal policy should even attempt to constrain union power. There is probably even less agreement on exactly how to do it.

The issue of government regulation of intraunion affairs is also of relatively late vintage. Efforts to protect wage earners from unions have not always been successful. Whether government should develop rules for the conduct of internal affairs of unions continues to be an issue of controversy.

U.S. Supreme Court opinions going back several decades have accommodated inherent tension between antitrust and labor law by finding an implied exemption in the antitrust laws for collective action during negotiations leading to a labor contract. This is now known as the doctrine of "non-statutory labor exemption." Without violating this doctrine, the Supreme Court in 1996 ruled in favor of employers, that it is not an antitrust violation for companies within an industry to get together and impose new contract terms on their unionized employees after labor negotiations have broken down.[1]

Unions in the United States, in effect, have served to provide their members with a sense of power against arbitrary behavior by employers. Membership grew rapidly during the period 1935–55. By 1955, one out of three nonfarm workers belonged to unions. In the four decades since 1955, however, the number belonging to unions declined so that only about one in six nonfarm workers were union members.

A major source of power for unions has always been the strike. The potential cost of a strike to employers, but also to employees, is usually an incentive to avoid it. It should thus be no surprise that agreement in most collective bargaining contracts in the Untied States has come about without resort to a strike. In a real sense, union power to raise the wages of their members without encouraging unemployment depends first on the availability of substitutes for their services. Second, the demand for products so produced must have few or preferably no substitutes; third, union member services should be but a small share of total cost; and fourth, the supply of any substitutes should be limited.[2]

On balance, unions and their members operating in the aforementioned environment have managed to raise earnings. Others not so favored have had little or no effect on the earnings of their members. The gains that unions have acquired probably came at the expense of consumers and/or nonunion workers. The available evidence suggests that unions have not increased the share of American national income going to labor.

The pricing route for an increase in real wages is by increase in productivity. Artificial increases in wages, whether by unions and/or government fiat, as discussed previously in the example of minimum wages, do little if anything to enhance worker productivity. It is possible that such actions may retard worker productivity.

One case favoring intervention does come to mind, however: A monopsony (a single producer) may be able to profit by restricting employment and paying a wage rate below the marginal revenue product created by the labor in question. It is possible to set a minimum wage, whether by a union or government, that at least theoretically will result in both higher wages and increased employment.

UNIONS AND FLEXIBILITY

Changing world circumstances pose serious problems, but also opportunities for unions. The problems are clear enough. In the United States, union membership increased slightly between 1993 and 1995 due to an increase in such membership in the public sector. Less than 11 percent of private sector workers are now in unions. Union political power has also declined in the United States since the 1950s. Much the same is true in Europe, where social democratic parties have been putting distance between themselves and unions.

Changes such as decentralization of wage systems in countries where centralization was formerly in place (e.g., Australia, France, Italy, New Zealand, Sweden) have reduced union influence. The exception is Germany, where the practice, although fraying, continues. In the United States, such centralized wage systems are not common practice.

Another change working to weaken union influence is probably the difficulty in organizing small plants or firms. It is easier and cheaper, for instance, to organize a 500-worker plant than, say, a 50-worker plant. World-wide, the trend is for a smaller plant size, and so some observers note that it is no surprise that union membership has also fallen.

In general, unions all over the world are at a loss when asked how they intend to organize workers in private sector service firms. Organizers in many of the industrial unions, accustomed as they are to assembly-line workers, are simply at a loss when dealing with, say, library workers, secretaries, and laboratory technicians. The dialogue between the organizer and potential union member is at best likely to be confused. It may be necessary for unions to think harder about what it is they are trying to sell to their potential customers or members. For instance, unions may need to go beyond promoting their principal product of collective wage bargaining. Some European unions are now pushing nonwage issues such as regulation of part-time work, parental leave, and related issues. Other unions provide, among other things, advice on discipline, grievances, and legal assistance.

Some observers note that since nonpay concerns weigh heavily on workers in service industries, including knowledge industries, unions may promote themselves as service providers to individuals rather than collectives.[3] As a result, unions may evolve into something resembling the craft guilds of medieval times. It is interesting to note that people once wondered whether these guilds could adapt to industrialization. The survival of contemporary unions may depend on the lessons from their craft-based origins.[4] Certainly, if unions view their job as the prevention of change, they will fall by the wayside.

THE ISSUE OF LABOR EFFICIENCY AND WELFARE

It is now almost taken for granted that a country's prosperity and development depend more on knowledge and the technical skills and diligence of its labor force than on the size and quality of capital and natural resources. As a result, attention is focused on those public policies that increase the efficiency of labor.

Tt is important to distinguish the concept of the efficiency of labor from its productivity. The efficiency of labor means attributes of labor such as skills, training, diligence, and flexibility. The productivity of labor, on the other hand, means the ratio of output to labor; it is usually expressed as output per man-year, per mean-hour, or some other relevant measure. For example, the productivity of labor increases if the amount of plant and equipment used with the labor increases, all other things remaining equal.

The impediments to labor efficiency are also well documented and known. They include widespread ignorance, rigid taboos, class structures and family arrangements, and social institutions. Singly or in combination, such barriers serve to block or dampen efforts to advance the efficiency of labor. Fortunately for the United States, social and cultural forms and forces favor long-run increases in labor efficiency. Social attitudes in the United Staets are dynamic and welcome change. Nevertheless, there is still much ignorance, prejudice, and superstition in the United States.

It is also important to keep in mind that improvements in the efficiency of labor or, more broadly, human resources should be welcomed for their own sake. The purpose of a country's development should serve its population. Human resources, and improvements in its quality and efficiency, is the end of and not simply the means to development.

Health and education of the population are welcome. America's population is not simply an instrument to be improved for the transcendent ends of the country apart from its people. Few in the United States would agree that human beings are a means only. Unfortunately, many discussions are carried on as though people are simply the means to an end.

Consider the relation between education and economic growth. It is assumed that more years of education for the population translate into increases in economic growth. Certainly, a relationship exists. Exactly how education promotes economic growth is difficult to gauge with precision. How many more dollars expended on education will produce how much more future economic growth is something we will probably never know.

For many years in the post–World War II era, economic growth was used to justify ever increasing investments in education. In fact, the Cold War years and concerns with Soviet military and political strength underscored education as a requisite for economic growth. These developments served to strengthen attempts to improve the efficiency of labor. At the same time, they also strengthened the view that leads to viewing human beings as if they were means, not ends.

This concern with economic growth led to attempts to show that social welfare measures also promote growth. Many of the programs put in place during these years (e.g., public health, subsidies for medical research, vocational training, public assistance, unemployment compensation) may have raised the efficiency of labor. All these programs can be called investments in human resources. The problem is that attempts to quantify such investments and their returns may easily slip into treating human beings as means, not ends.

Observers note, however, that American weakness does lie in people skills, including education and training. How should the government respond? The obvious route is to improve education and training. This may raise taxes, which will raise costs elsewhere in the economy. In any case, such improvements are likely to take years to be realized.

Nevertheless, the social consequences that occur as a result of weak education and training include a low-paid underclass that will become increasingly unacceptable. European governments have used minimum wages to prevent pay from falling at the end of the jobs scale. As we have discussed, this attempt to protect living standard via minimum wages will likely cost some workers their jobs. A better way for governments to reduce inequalities could be through income supplements for the low paid. The difficulty is to avoid eroding the incentive to work, which would create an unemployment trap. This, of course, demands that the withdrawal of benefits as incomes rise is gradual. Any such arrangement could prove to be expensive.

In America, a growing low-paid underclass contains both white and blacks. In this sense, whites and blacks share common, converging interests. When it comes to strengthening education and training and so removing some pockets of blight that blemish American society, race may not be a very useful concept.

It is thus not surprising that many people have pressed for protection against competition from low-wage countries. Such competition is viewed as destroying jobs, lowering living standards, and encouraging the growth of a low-paid underclass in America. These concerns are at the center of opposition in the United States to the North American Free Trade Agreement (NAFTA) with Mexico and Canada. Average wages in the United States are seven times those in Mexico. Some American politicians underscore that removal of trade barriers between the two countries would move American jobs to Mexico.

Appealing as the argument may be, it ignores the fact that the productivity of the average American worker is higher than that of the average Mexican. In effect, labor costs per unit of output vary by much less than pay differentials alone would suggest. As long as American workers possess better skills and use better technology, they can compete, despite enjoying higher wages. With open borders, Mexico will acquire the latest technologies and labor productivity will rise. We have it from both theory and practice that this will be essentially matched either by a wage rise or rise in its exchange rate or by some of both. So-called cheap foreign Mexican labor will not displace American workers out of their jobs, simply because the world's output is not fixed. Free trade, in fact, opens new opportunities and so helps all parties.

It is a basic principle of economics, called comparative advantage, that a country should specialize in industries where it possesses such advantage. For America, this advantage is in building aircraft and other high-skill and high-technology goods and services. It should export such products and import, say, Mexico's cheaper goods. The net effect is to boost the export earnings of Mexico and so its imports of skill-intensive goods from America.

It is not, as protectionists argue, that the slow rate at which American living standards have risen over the past few years because the increase in imports. A more likely reason may well be America's low investment and cpmseqiemt slow productivity growth. Rich countries will gain as a whole from increased trade with emerging countries. Average living standards will rise faster. It is also true, however, that some groups of workers, especially unskilled ones, will likely lose out.

Also available from the economist's tool kit is the factor-price equalization theorem to gauge how free trade affects different workers' wages. This theorem predicts that trade will reduce the relative income of the type of labor, whether skilled or unskilled, that is relatively scarce in a country. Thus, if the United States, where unskilled labor is relatively scarce and skilled labor more abundant, trades with Mexico, where the labor scarcities are opposite, then the United States will specialize in skill-intensive industries and import the less skill-intensive goods from Mexico. As a result, America's output of skill-intensive goods and services will increase and its output of low-skill-intensive goods and services will decline. One consequence of these developments is that the demand for unskilled workers in the United States will decline, and so will their wages relative to those of skilled workers. By contrast, the wages of unskilled Mexican workers will rise.

The existing empirical evidence is consistent with the theory. As imports from the emerging countries such as Mexico increase, so the pay gap between skilled and unskilled workers in the United States has widened. For instance, in the 1980s the wages of the top 10 percent of male earners, in general the most highly skilled, has risen 20 percent relative to the bottom 10 percent earners, who are predominantly unskilled. This trend continues into the 1990s.

Moreover, wages of American male college graduates rose about 30 percent relative to those males with twelve or fewer years of education. Many American low-skilled workers suffered a real wage cut of about 13 percent in the 1980s. As expected, the least educated American workers also suffered the highest increase in unemployment.

It is apparent that the globalization of trade has tied the fate of developed industrial countries to that of the emerging countries. The decline in trade barriers and lower communication and transportation costs have worked in favor of globalization. So too has the improvement in educational standards in the poorer countries, thereby increasing the number of workers capable of participating and dealing with up-to-date technology.

Increased trade may be one contributor to the dwindling demand for unskilled workers in the United States. Another factor is surely technology, including computers, robots, and other equipment, which now do the repetitive tasks previously performed by unskilled workers. There is every reason to expect that the future holds more of the same. Demand in the United States and other industrial countries will inevitably shift further away from low-skilled workers in favor of skilled workers.

Government response to these developments should not be to increase trade barriers and subsidies to protect low skilled industries. Protectionism may protect and help low-skilled workers, but it will likely be at the expense of other workers. A case in point is that fewer jobs will be created in the more efficient industries.

Using taxpayer money for public works and job subsidies is not likely to provide a serious long-run solution to the declining demand for unskilled labor. Placing taxes on skill-intensive jobs for the sake of preserving low-skill jobs is a wrong approach. This will simply make the skill-intensive industries less profitable.

If education and training are improved so that the supply of unskilled workers is reduced, there will be less concern about low-skilled jobs. This raises an important issue: How easy is it to upgrade the skills of, say, middle-aged workers with limited education? Would the resources necessary for such upgrading be better used on new entrants to the labor force? The human suffering of those who lack skills is not always taken into account. This, as we discussed earlier, raises the issue of whether human beings are a means or end of economic activity. The challenge here is how to compensate the losers through some combination of training and government assistance without damaging incentives to work.

Available evidence from American national unemployment statistics indicate that black workers, blue-collar workers, and less-educated workers are disproportionately represented in these data. The chronically unemployed are more likely to be blue-collar workers and are more likely to have no more than a high school education. However, a considerable number of other workers who do not have these characteristics are also among the chronically unemployed. The fact is that for a small group of prime-age (thirty-five to sixty-four years) workers, unemployment constitutes a recurring and serious blight on their lives. Thus, while unemployment is an infrequent or short-lived affair for most Americans, it is a common and often financially tragic affair for a small group of people in the economy.

Again, some observers suggest that for the chronically unemployed, government policy can be designed to assist these people. One policy would include devices designed to promote stable employment for them. This is the reasoning behind government personnel training programs. The difficulty is that few of the chronically unemployed are attracted to such programs. In any case, available evidence suggests that the effect of these programs in raising the earnings of trainees apparently does not extend much beyond a short time after the training period.

It is possible that a policy of providing employment subsidies to firms would be helpful, and given the present structure of taxes on business, this could be accomplished by reducing payroll taxes. The evidence suggests, however, that tax incentives as accelerated depreciation allowances and investment tax credits tend to benefit highly skilled workers more than low-skilled workers so that, partly to neutralize these regressive effects, various schemes have been advanced to provide subsidies to firms that increase their employment from some base level. The problem is that these subsidies would have to be highly skewed toward low-wage workers.

Another policy for dealing with the chronically unemployed is simply to provide them and their families with the necessary income to meet their basic physiological needs. Such a policy would replace the present welfare programs with a comprehensive income maintenance system that provides a guaranteed minimum income for all families, whether or not members of these families are at work in the labor market. Studies have computed the work incentive effects that have measured the budgetary costs of such programs.[5] The results suggest that, provided such programs substituted rather than augmented the present welfare system, the costs appear reasonable.

Various proposals to reform the American welfare system are always up for discussion. In 1996, for instance, Michigan and Wisconsin pushed proposals for a vast overhaul of welfare programs. Their central provision would mandate work in exchange for benefits. These states are in the forefront of efforts for a vast change in national policy that would end welfare's status as a federal entitlement and grant the states, with virtually no strings, the authority to design and administer their own programs.

Some states, such as Michigan, with federal government approval, proceeded with their own experiments, imposing restrictions on welfare beneficiaries and creating work incentives. Both Michigan and Wisconsin move welfare policy in the same direction. They require nearly all welfare recipients to work, and they quickly cut off benefits to those who did not. But the Michigan plan stops short of Wisconsin's proposal, which would not guarantee a job and could leave even those who qualify for benefits without government aid.

The specifics of the Michigan proposal suggests a carrot-and-stick approach to welfare. Thus, Michigan would cut off welfare benefits and food stamps within 60 days to recipients who refused to take a job offered or, if no job was available, to those who refused to perform community service work or enroll in job-training programs. However, Michigan would guarantee access to health care, transportation, and child care for those who participated in the program. Michigan would also pay to continue Medicaid benefits for one year for welfare recipients who find jobs in the private sector but lack health insurance. The state's welfare case load has dropped significantly in the period 1994–96. It is not clear, however, whether the drop can be attributed to the program or to the improved economic climate in Michigan in the same period.[6]

PRODUCTIVITY OF LABOR AND CAPITAL

Many observers argue that one of America's main problems is flagging productivity growth. Over the past two decades, productivity growth has been behind the complaint that American living standards are slipping.

The importance of productivity to living standards is clear enough. The idea is simple. Productivity is measured by dividing the total output of goods and services in different sectors by the number of man-hours it took to produce them. Rising productivity means that worker output per hour is on the upswing. As a consequence, worker compensation should also increase.

American data indicate that average productivity grew by almost 3 percent a year between 1960 and 1973. In the years between 1973 and 1996, the annual average growth of productivity declined to about 1.1 percent. The fact is that other industrial countries also slowed, but not as much as the American rate.

Several explanations have been put forth. One is that America was so far ahead of other countries in the postwar period that those countries have been catching up in the past few years. If this is correct, there is little that the United States can do about it.

Another explanation is that increasing investment by providing labor with more capital and equipment tends to increase productivity. Since Europe and Japan apparently invest more heavily than America, the solution for America's problem is to invest more and so raise productivity.

Still another possibility is that America's productivity problem is really a nonissue. It could be that available productivity estimates are incorrect. Much of the country's output is now in services, where output performance and so productivity is much harder to estimate. Not surprisingly, available estimates on low productivity in America may simply be fictitious.

Still other observers note that in addition to the measurement problem, the slow growth in services can also be attributed to the structure of America's labor market. Due to the relatively (by comparison to Europe) low real wages at the bottom of the labor market, many service firms—such as restaurants, shopping mall outlets, and other related firms—have many more workers than their European counterparts. The slow overall growth of productivity in these American sectors, observers note, is, in part, the mirror image of high unemployment in Europe.[7]

There is little doubt that unsatisfactory labor productivity in important services is the area where governments should consider proper policies to raise such productivity. The obvious policy candidate to increase investment is to encourage saving and promote investment in skills. It is not at all clear that many governments have been effective in promoting such policies.

Another area of concern is capital productivity, which is also hard to measure. Evidence suggests that American firms make far better use of their physical capital than either Germany or Japan.[8] For the entire business sector, a unit of capital input in Germany or Japan generates output that is about one third below that of a unit of capital in the United States.

The difficulties in measuring capital productivity are even more formidable than for labor productivity. Labor productivity can be roughly measured by the number of hours workers work. Capital productivity estimates, however, must combine the values of a wide range of capital goods, such as machines, buildings, and so forth. In addition, how much of the economy's capital stock is used up during a given period must also be estimated. A simple method advanced by some analysts is to assume that a physical asset will last for a given period of time. For instance, if it lasts ten years, then 10 percent of its value counts as capital input each year. Obviously, such estimates are rough indeed. Little wonder that few analysts readily accept each other's capital productivity estimates.

What is particularly interesting in the results reported in these studies of capital productivity is that America manages to create more wealth than Germany and Japan, even though it saves and invests less. For instance, between 1974 and 1993, gross domestic savings in the United States averaged 25 percent of the GDP compared with 31 percent for Germany and 36 percent for Japan. Nevertheless, the United States created $26,500 of new wealth per person (in 1993 prices) as measured by households' net financial wealth, while Germany created $21,900 and Japan $20,900.

These reports suggest that, in part, the answer lies with America's high capital productivity, which in turn generated higher financial returns. It is estimated that in the United States, industry managed a 9 percent return on capital between 1974 and 1993, while in Japan and Germany, the return was about 7 percent for the same period.

Reasons for the better performance of capital in the United States include management styles, capital and financial markets, and regulation. Thus, management styles are reflected in the way Americans run their companies, including finance and marketing products and services. The stronger pressure from investors forces American managers to focus on financial performance, which tends to make them very careful in selecting investment projects. Moreover, the low entry (and exit) barriers and intense competition force American firms to make the best possible use of their capital. In Germany and Japan, on the other hand, many poorly performing firms are protected by various government regulations.

Both Germany and Japan are moving in the direction of making their economies more competitive, and so more in tune with the current globalization of economic activity. Parliament in Germany, for instance, approved a major part of an austerity plan in June 1996 that would reduce workers' sick pay and job security in an effort to increase the competitiveness of the nation's industry.[9] According to the German sponsors of the plan, the idea is to cut the country's labor costs, already among the world's highest, by almost $50 billion by the end of the decade. Opposition to the plan is widespread among Germany's workers, who argue that the government's austerity measures punish workers while making no demands on their employers. Perhaps the intent is to use more labor-intensive production methods, thereby gaining some capital productivity at the expense of labor productivity. German labor productivity is about 80 percent of that for the United States in the period 1990–93.

It is important to keep a proper perspective on all these events and their bearing on globalization. After all, globalization is nothing new. In fact, for a good many years before World War I, national economies became more closely linked due to declining transportation costs, among other factors. The collapse of the interwar world economy reduced the drive toward globalization. In the post–World War II period, and particularly since the fall of communism, the drive toward globalization again sped up. Theoretically, we should expect that global integration will adversely affect a country's relatively scarce factors of production. The scarce factor in industrial countries is low-skilled labor, relative to the more abundant low-skilled labor in emerging economies of Asia and other areas.

NOTES

1. See Linda Greenhouse, "Justices Grant U.S. Employers Tool to Bargain," *The New York Times*, Friday, June 21, 1996, p. A1.

2. On these and related issues, see H. Gregg Lewis, *Unionism and Relative Wages in the United States* (Chicago: University of Chicago Press, 1963), and Alfred Marshall, *Principles of Economics*, 8th ed. (New York: Macmillan, 1920).

3. For a discussion of these issues, see "Trade Unions," *The Economist* (July 1, 1996), 336:7921, pp. 54–56.

4. Ibid., p. 56.

5. See, for instance, M. C. Keeley, P. K. Robins, R. G. Spiegelman, and R. W. West, "The Labor Supply Effects and Costs of Alternative Negative Income Tax Programs," *Journal of Human Resources* (Winter 1978), 13:1, pp. 3–36.

6. Many of the welfare reforms now gaining popularity were discussed by Milton Friedman many years ago. See, for instance, William R. Allen, ed., *Milton Friedman:*

Bright Promises Dismal Performance: An Economist's Protest (New York: Harcourt Brace Jovanovich, 1983).

7. "A Working Hypothesis," *The Economist* (May 11, 1996), 339:7965, p. 74.

8. "America's Power Plants," *The Economist* (June 8, 1996), 339:7969, p. 82.

9. See Alan Cowell, "Austerity Plan for Workers Is Approved in Germany," *The New York Times*, Saturday, June 29, 1996, pp. 17–18.

Chapter 10

The Prospects of American
Economic Policy

ECONOMIC POLICY: COMPLEX STRUCTURE OF ENDS AND MEANS

The prospects of economic policy contain the large problems of the whole American economy. These include globalization, inflation, unemployment, low incomes, lagging growth, and the like. It is clear that more than economic logic is needed for the solutions of problems through government policy. Pressure groups will always exert a strong influence on American policy.

Consider first the issue of globalization. There is now a consensus that argues that globalization has considerably diminished the power of governments to steer their economies.[1] Even with the growth of capital flows, however, governments retain discretion in economic policy. None of the Group of Seven countries, least of all the United States, has any intention of surrendering sovereignty to the Group for the purpose that put group interests ahead of national ones.[2]

The 1996 summit of the Group of Seven (United States, Japan, Germany, France, Britain, Italy, and Canada) big industrial countries has prompted discussion of whether policy coordination is possible or even desirable, and whether the Group is the right forum.[3] The frictions among the countries are clear enough. Germany's desire for frugality and France's penchant for bureaucratic coordination of national policies are well known. America's interests in bilateral trade and regional cooperation are also clear and serve to undermine multilateralism and freer trade.

For instance, America's trade officials present their policy toward Japan as a means of remedying the country's current account deficit—a position they know to be economically indefensible. Indeed, to the extent that Japan increases imports from America at the expense of exporters in other countries, this is trade discrimination. Of course, this is the opposite of the free trade America claims to seek.

American government responsibility for developing policy toward trade, stability, growth, and full employment is now taken for granted. Solutions to these difficult problems will be attempted as usual through the joint efforts of government, business, and labor. The difficulty is that public discussion of economic policy is nearly always on short-run issues and/or their short-run aspects and consequences. To this may be added the differences of opinion and of social and economic philosophy.

Any serious analysis must first frame its problem clearly. After all, a problem is something that calls for solution. If deviation from an ideal economy constitutes a problem to be solved by an act of economic policy, then a multitude of problems, large and small, exist. Consider again the example of the international trade problem. Most people will agree that it is a serious problem. If it is not solved, what then? The answer is that waste of resources, of some unknown amount, will continue; but the waste has been tolerated in the American economy for some time, partly because the waste, though a cost to consumers, taxpayers, and others is, after all, income to many. If that trade problem should be solved, would not the solution cause others problems (e.g., unemployment in the American automobile industry)? It is with good reason that the notion of a problem should be approached carefully.

As we have discussed, the preservation and promotion of competition in the American economy is a serious problem. It is serious because there are many factors and interests determined to weaken it. Competition is essential because it is the means toward the unquestioned objectives of efficiency for the entire economy as well as for the preservation of free American institutions.

The importance of economic stability is continually underscored. Ever since the 1930s, America's concern with employment and price stability is clear. Concern with welfare and poverty has changed over the years. Low incomes and pockets of poverty persist. The problem is to marshal the economic, social, and political technologies and methods that will contribute to the elimination of pockets of poverty without damaging to the incentives to work.

For all the problems discussed, there are government economic policies in place. The fact that the issues are labeled as problems underscores the belief that existing policies are not completely satisfactory. There is every reason to believe that they will continue to be less than satisfactory. There are at least two reasons for this view. There is, first, the need for compromise among the ends of economic policy. The second reason is the existence of interest groupings who do not agree on what ends to pursue or what compromises to make. If there is only one problem and one goal to be reached, solutions will readily come forth. The difficulty is that there are always many problems.

It is thus not surprising that the ends of economic policy are pursued rather than achieved. Any agreement in an analysis of the relations among the primary ends of stability, employment, growth, efficiency, and freedom is unlikely, because the ends are subject to complete and agreeable quantification of benefits and costs.

At least three of the primary ends of economic policy can be expressed quantitatively, however roughly. Stability, as indicated by various measures of price indexes, output, and employment, can be useful provided that we do not insist on accurate measures. Much the same is also true for growth, as indicated by a percentage rate of increase of real output per capita per year. The problem becomes even more difficult when attempts are made to measure the efficiency of resource allocation. How does one place a quantity value on freedom?

It is also important to keep in mind the ends of economic policy over time. In the pre-Depression years of the 1920s, stability meant price stability; in the 1930s, the focus shifted to employment. In the post–World War II years, stability probably meant stable, price-growing full employment. In these years, forces on growth stressed increasing America's stock of technologically advanced capital equipment and related items.

On more than one occasion in this book, we have indicated conflicts between pairs of objectives. The illustration of inflation and employment is but one case in point. Others come readily to mind: full employment versus growth, competition versus collective labor union bargaining. In effect, concentration on any one primary end could mean failure to achieve other ends.

As for the difficult problem of raising the standards of economic policy (standards that would mean workable agreement on the importance of the ends of policies and on the use of means), the skeptics may be correct in their view that not much improvement is likely. The various competing interests are able to distort the structure of policy to make it serve their particular interest with damage to the general national interest. In essence, can the various conflicting interests transcend group interests for the benefit of national interest and thus raise the standards of economic policy? There is already broad agreement on certain standards or principles, such as competition, collective bargaining, and government responsibility for stability. However, as long as the various economic interest groups are free to pursue their own short-run self-interests, policy conflicts are likely.

It is little wonder that foreigners are often confused when dealing with the inconsistencies of American economic policies. They note that various inconsistencies in American policies such as international trade and anti-trust hamper the country in its role as one of the world's leading nations.

For all its postwar progress, foreign economic policy in the United States still has not attained the stature of, say, Great Britain's in the nineteenth century. Ideas on foreign trade are still influenced by mercantilist thought and policies of almost three centuries ago. Received theory has long demonstrated the logic of the gains of international free trade as a long-range policy. Due to pressure groups, however, America has always had something less than free trade in place.

Present and future economic policy, including foreign economic policy, continues to be a complex structure of ends and means. There are both long-range and short-range political-economic and economic objectives. Quite simply, they do not form a consistent or an integrated form. Authority over the various means of policy is characteristically divided among the legislative and several executive branches of the federal government.

Consider, for instance, the problem of recent immigration to the United States. For a long time, economic, social, and political policy has focused on whether heavy immigration is a burden and threat or an overall benefit to the economy. The conclusions of recent studies tend to confirm the fear that immigration may indeed be a burden and perhaps even a threat.[4] The results suggest that the economic success of immigrants varies sharply, with Mexicans and Central Americans lagging even further behind their counterparts from Europe and Asia, as well as behind native-born Americans. As usual, policy prescription is unclear.

As a nation of immigrants, Americans are reluctant, it is argued, to close the doors to new immigrants. Some evidence suggests that recent immigrants tend to earn more after a few years than Americans. Still other evidence indicates that the economic quality of immigrants fell sharply in the 1960s with the tide of largely poor and uneducated arrivals from Latin America. The wage gap between Latin American immigrants and native-born workers actually widens as both groups gain experience in the American job market. For example, economic assimilation is eluding a lot of Mexicans, who make up 21 percent of the immigration counted in the American 1990 census.

The evidence does cast doubt on the contribution to the American economy by Latin American immigrants. Due to their efforts, some products produced in the United States may now be less expensive, but the competition has exacerbated the problems of low-skilled native workers already hard hit in the labor market. Evidence suggests that immigration has lowered the wages of native-born high-school dropouts by roughly a third.

To these objections can also be added that immigrants are a burden on social services. Limited though the evidence may be, it is correct that poor legal immigrants, like other poor Americans, are more likely to make use of the various welfare programs in place. Little wonder that many people want a more selective immigration policy favoring highly skilled applicants. Again pressure groups, pro- and anti-immigration, largely talk past each other, refusing to acknowledge that multifaced problems demand a sophisticated and rational public policy.

Immigration and globalization pose serious challenges since both political and economic effects of a decision may run in the same direction or may clash. Globalization may hurt owners of a country's relatively scarce resource, which, in America, is low-skilled workers. Pressure to restrict immigration owes much to the fears of the low-skilled workers that may lose from globalization. Such fears are borne out by the predictions of standard economic theory.

Another ready example of public policy conflicts and the influence of various and diverse pressure groups is the use of economic sanctions. There is now a practice in America of elevating economic sanctions to the status of an instrument of warfare. Economic sanctions are simply not an effective weapon of political warfare.[5] In fact, they are more likely to do more harm to the United States than to the intended target country. They serve to weaken the system of free markets that American policy promotes and that is the country's greatest source of strength. Their use is a confession of impotence.

Economic sanctions in the complex of several foreign economic policies may serve to complicate problems elsewhere in the economy. The United States, for instance, may not be the only country producing the goods at issue. The end result may be to push American producers to incur losses without any tangible gains. If these are products of American industries already in difficulty for other reasons, the net effect will be to hasten their deadline.

Although foreign aid is no longer as prominent as it once was in the American economy, it does merit attention if only to underscore the degree to which there is much pushing and pulling by various pressure groups. Foreign aid makes dollars available to foreigners. It is an unusually complex group of problems. The objectives are multiple and shifting, and so are the techniques.

Some of America's stated objectives in the postwar period since 1945 are economic recovery of potentially strong allies, military aid, and the encouragement of growth of underdeveloped areas of the world. These objectives have been pursued in sequence, and some of them in the same periods. Given the changing international situation confronting America, we can expect changes in the amounts, objectives, and direction of foreign aid.

Pressures on the various aid programs come from Congress, administrators of many of the programs, and from the missionary spirit now expressed in the secular language of the humanitarian impulse. Still other people have pushed these programs as a way to gain the goodwill, if not the gratitude, of other nations. Much is expected from American dollars.

The various foreign aid programs undertaken by the United States have been aimed at several political and economic objectives, both short range and long range. It is thus hopeless to look for any single clear standard of evaluation. Single projects can be evaluated by economic criteria of their expected benefits and costs. But programs that consist of many individual projects are much more difficult to evaluate. For instance, if foreign aid programs contribute to the economic growth of other nations, they meet one test of success. Economic growth, however, may be accompanied by increased dependence on imports and so lead to balance-of-payments problems, which, in turn, lead to new demands for economic aid from America. Economic growth may lead to political unrest, independence, and possibly to political behavior inconsistent with the aims of foreign aid.

In the past, the United States has often come into conflict with the recipient countries of foreign aid over private investment. The United States has attempted to foster private investment in the recipient nations along with its public grants and loans. Many of these countries have tended to be hostile to private industries. There is reason to believe that with the collapse of socialism, hostility to the private investor has declined.

Clearly, all segments of the economy influence each other, and decisions in each field of economic policy necessarily affect operations of other fields of economic policy. It is simple enough to indicate the ways in which foreign economic policy can be integrated with major domestic economic policies. Thus, the promotion of economic growth would include stress on greater and much freer foreign trade. America's economy would become more efficient by taking greater advantage of international specialization. The less efficient industries would decline as resources are transferred to the more efficient industries. Investment opportunities would expand with freer foreign trade. It is also clear that restrictive foreign trade policies would conflict with growth policies.

A more competitive policy that removes barriers to trade harmonizes with the objectives of American anti-trust laws just as restrictive policies clash. Imports can be used to increase the effectiveness of competition in domestic industries. Export subsidies, on the other hand, are short-range policies that are in conflict with the long-range objectives of economic growth policies.

Policies for economic stability are now much more closely tied to foreign economic policy than was formerly the case. Globalization has served to promote the tie between domestic economic stability and external events.

GOVERNMENT INFLUENCE ON THE ECONOMY

It is useful to put policies into broad groups based on their intended and actual effects on the American private enterprise economy.

Selected economic controls, for instance, can strengthen the operation of a private enterprise economy. The most notable are, of course, antitrust laws that promote and preserve competition. They are also likely to be resented by some businesspeople who see such laws as an unwarranted interference in the normal conduct of business affairs. Nevertheless, strong antitrust laws capably enforced do promote and pressure competition.

This is also true of government supervision of the monetary and financial organization. There are, however, reservations in the ways and means such supervision of these organizations is exercised. The preservation of monetary and price stability is absolutely essential to the effective and efficient functioning of a private enterprise economy. Failure to do so will result in significant losses to producers, consumers, savers, and investors.

Regulations aimed at specific private activity, such as various financial practices and regulation of food and drugs, put the government into the roles of arbiter, mediator, and policeofficer. The idea, of course, is not to limit the total of private enterprise. It is rather to channel such activities to reduce the likelihood of conflict.

In the event of natural or other disasters, the government provides emergency help. Such help takes the form of loans, grants, use of physical facilities, and even military assistance. There are the unexceptional instances when government bails out the nearly bankrupt or bankrupt, as in the case of the savings and loan industry. There is always the possibility that what began as an emergency or temporary government measure of assistance may become permanent. The concern is that such measures, if permanent, will undermine competition. In fact, government, emergency loans can result in expansion of government ownership, as has been the case in some countries.

In some industries such as public utilities and transportation, government policy may substitute rate making for competition. Although the companies are private, they do include public power projects. The net result is a mixture of public controls and private enterprise, with the usual difficulties that such a combination yields.

There are government policies that simply interfere wotj and obstruct the operation of natural market forces. This book discusses several, including minimum wages, sanctions, tariffs, subsidies, and the like. The policies serve to alter the allocation of resources in the production and consumption of such products and services. There is little, if any, coordination of such policies. They are far more responsive to private pressure groups than to the public interest.

For a good many years, labor legislation in the United States was considered as contrary to the freedom of the individual and to the natural forces of the market. Since the Great Depression of the 1930s, a change in attitude has occurred among those who might otherwise be inclined to oppose labor legislation. Labor organizations are now viewed as important elements in the American economy.

The same is true for the various social insurance systems now in place in the United States. They are now considered compatible with a private enterprise economy. Social insurance arrangements can serve to strengthen a private enterprise economy by removing the worst fears of labor regarding unemployment and illness.

In addition to the aforementioned government influences on the economy, there is a great range of services that are essentially indivisible and that must be produced by the government. Services such as defense, highways, and the like are an illustration. There are also services that the government produces in direct or indirect competition with private enterprise. The U.S. Post Office is an example, as well as various government insurance arrangements.

POTENTIAL POLICY PROBLEMS

It is, of course, difficult to identify precisely future problems that will demand policy action on the part of governments. some likely areas for concern include Social Security, welfare, health care, the environment, energy, and defense.

Consider Social Security and welfare. Everyone agrees that both the Social Security and welfare systems can and should be effectively designed and operated. Many will agree that the welfare system is a bureaucratic nightmare. They will also agree that the Social Security system has expanded enormously. It is likely that both the Social Security and welfare systems contain major work disincentives that serve to reduce or retard the country's total national output.

In the case of Social Security, there is concern that current retirees are receiving benefits many times the amount in taxes paid in. Some people feel that these are intergenerational transfers for which there is little, if any, justification. Accordingly, this redistribution feature of the system is really its major activity. In essence, young working people are transferring large sums of money to old people, some of whom may be rich. The result may be that some people are receiving an enormous windfall from the Social Security system. If not corrected soon, so the argument goes, the system is headed for serious trouble.

The welfare system, as noted elsewhere in this book, leaves much to be desired. Welfare coverage, as well as benefit levels, varies greatly from state to state. Within states, there is egregious unequal treatment of identically selected families. Even when the law is uniformly administered, two equally situated poor families may receive very different levels of support. There is also the unfair treatment of similar but not identical families. Thus, a working family may end up with significantly less income than a nonworking family. In addition, there are also outright cases of fraud.

Considerable concern is expressed by various experts about the need to restore the Medicare trust fund to financial solvency into the next century when the so-called baby boomers retire. According to various estimates, Medicare's Part A trust fund, which finances hospital care, will become insolvent in 2001, one year earlier than previously predicted. Part A's slippage is attributed to health costs (which drive spending) rising faster than wage increases. This is certainly bad news because Part A's revenues are tied to the payroll tax. When wages do not rise, neither do revenues.

Moreover, Social Security's trust fund will be depleted by 2029, according to projections made in 1995. Various proposals are forthcoming, complete with political baggage. These include limiting the amount Medicare can spend each year. Another is to make the health care system more efficient. This concept lies behind the congressional support for managed care, which includes health maintenance organizations. In any case, long-term solutions for the stability of Social Security, Medicare, or Medicaid are going to be serious challenges for government policies.

American environmental policy is in need of repair. In fact, the country's environment is still deteriorating.[6] Pressure on some sensitive habitats continues to grow; population density in coastal regions has risen nearly 70 percent since 1970. Municipal waste is taking on crisis proportions in America. Indeed, Americans dump more garbage than any other people on earth. Nuclear waste and used nuclear fuel pile up in temporary stores. Traffic on American roads in 1996 was double the amount of traffic in 1970. The United States remains the world's largest producer of carbon dioxide, which may be causing global warming.

Furthermore, the analysts report that total spending on environmental protection probably cost about 2 percent of the GDP in 1993. There is no evidence that such expenditures had a negative impact on national economic growth and the overall competitiveness of the private sector. Indeed, expenditures on environmental protection have created 4 million jobs and will probably add another 1 million by the end of the 1990s.

Such evidence will be useful to the Environmental Protection Agency, particularly in promoting various environmental programs and policies. Attempts by various pressure groups to cut environmental spending, especially on the Superfund used to clean up the worst pollution and on enforcement, are well known. Costs of regulations may be high as a result of unresolved and confused division of responsibilities among federal, state, and local governments.

There are also problems over significant subsidiess such as federal energy subsidiess which cost $5 billion to $10 billion in 1990. It could be that higher prices for water and energy should be considered as cost-effective ways to achieve environmental goals. The fact that antienvironmental pressure groups are pushing various policies suggests that once again environmental policy will become their hostage.

In discussing the energy crisis ofthe 1970s. Milton Friedman noted that the United States has an energy problem for the reason that the price mechanism has not been allowed to work by the country at home and by the Organization of Petroleum Exporting Countries (OPEC) cartel abroad.[7] OPEC was created as a monopoly and has raised the price of oil by keeping the amount available to the market down to the amount demanded at that price. In effect, Friedman attributed the energy problem to the cumulative effects of the OPEC cartel to government controls and regulations, and to the change in philosophical attitudes of the public toward government involvement in the energy area.

Friedman notes that there is no argument on economic grounds for having a Department of Energy, for having a Federal Energy Administration, or for having price controls, and there is almost no professional economist who will argue otherwise. Most economists are, in fact, in favor of the deregulation of oil and gas.

On defense policy and related issues, a lively debate can be counted on to continue. How the debate will go depends in part on the performance of the American economy and the state of Russia. A healthy economy and a healthy Russia make defense cuts easier to justify. Experts discount talk of a resurgent Russia, and if Russia did become a threat, it would be a threat to its neighbors before it threatened America. The Pentagon bureaucracy has emphasized regional security. Pointing to areas like the former Yugoslavia, Iraq, and Somalia, the Department of Defense says its goal is to make sure that American troops are able to reach trouble spots quickly with overwhelming power in order to deter—and, if needed, defeat—aggression with the help of allies and friends.

The Pentagon also wants to curb the proliferation of nuclear weapons and improve missile defense programs. Its budget requests also call for a combination of counterproliferation measures and continued efforts at nucleararms reduction.

The key issue and problem is how and why the United States should commit American lives and wealth to enforcing some vague and questionable new form of imperial order.[8] A debate continues between those peoples advocating a more moderate approach and others pushing for more defense outlays to restore American power and purpose.

It is simply not clear what purpose an increase over the $260 billion military outlay for 1996 will serve. Consider that America already accounts for almost 40 percent of all military spending on earth, as Bandow notes. The United States spends at least three times as much as Russia and twice as much as Germany, Britain, France, and Japan combined. It is simply inconceivable that America's allies are unable to handle security threats on their own.

The purpose of these vast expenditures becomes clear if we take some Republican analysts seriously. It is, in fact, nothing less than that the United States takes on itself the responsibility for policing the world. America is to meddle in civil wars (e.g., former Yugoslavia, Somalia, and so on), to restore order to broken and impossible societies, and to extend American security guarantees through NATO right up to Russia's frontier. In other words, America is being asked to accept some vague proposals about spending more on defense intended for some empire determined to establish hegemony over other people and countries. Surely this is not what most people want in the republic America purports to be, as Bandow correctly concludes.

NOTES

1. See George Macesich, *Integration and Stabilization: A Monetary View* (Westport, CT: Praeger, 1996).

2. For instance, see "Can the G7 Ride Again?" *The Economist* (June 22, 1996), 339:7971, p. 76.

3. Ibid., p.76.

4. See Peter Passell, "Economic Scene: Some Second Thoughts Arise on Benefits of Immigration," *The New York Times*, Thursday, July 4, 1996, p. C2.

5. See Milton Friedman, "Economic Sanctions," in William R. Allen, ed., *Milton Friedman: Bright Promises Dismal Performance: An Economist's Protest* (New York: Harcourt Brace Jovanovich, 1983), pp. 370–372.

6. See "Environmental Policy: Could Try Harder," *The Economist* (October 1995), 337:7937, pp. 32–33.

7. See Milton Friedman, "The Energy Crisis," in William R. Allen, ed., *Milton Friedman: Bright Promises Dismal Performance: An Economist's Protest* (New York: Harcourt Brace Jovanovich, 1983), pp. 141–152.

8. See Doug Bandow, "Dole's Military Card," *The New York Times*, Saturday, July 6, 1996, p. 15, for a discussion of several key issues in the defense budget and direction of policy.

Bibliography

Adams, Walter, and Horace M. Gray. *Monopoly in America: The Government as Promoter.* New York: Macmillian, 1955, p. 74.

Aiyagarai, S. Rao. "Response to a Defense of Zero Inflation." *Quarterly Review* (Spring 1991), Federal Reserve Bank of Minneapolis, pp. 21–24.

Allen, William R. (ed.). *Milton Friedman: Bright Promises Dismal Performance: An Economist's Protest.* New York: Harcourt Brace Jovanovich, 1983.

Arnowitz, Victor. "On the Accuracy and Properties of Recent Macroeconomic Forecasts." *American Economic Review* (May 1976), pp. 313–319.

Bandow, Doug. "Dole's Military Card." *The New York Times*, Saturday, July 6, 1996, p. 15.

Bernstein, Marver H. *Regulating Business by Independent Commission.* Princeton, NJ: Princeton University Press, 1955.

Bordo, M. D. "The Classical Gold Standard: Source Lessons from Today." *Monthly Review* (May 1981), Federal Reserve Bank of St. Louis, pp. 2–17.

Burns, Arthur Robert. *The Decline of Competition.* New York: McGraw-Hill, 1936.

Cagan, Phillip. "The Monetary Dynamics of Hyper Inflation." *Studies in the Quantity Theory of Money*, Milton Friedman (ed.). Chicago: University of Chicago Press, 1956, pp. 25–117.

Campbell, Colin D., and William R. Dougan (eds.). *Alternative Monetary Regimes.* Baltimore: The Johns Hopkins University Press, 1986.

Carlson, K. M. "Monetary and Fiscal Actions in Macroeconomic Models." *Review*, Federal Reserve Bank of St. Louis (January 1974), pp. 8–18.

Chamberlain, Edward H. *The Theory of Monopolistic Competition.* Cambridge: Harvard University Press, 1933.

Clark, M. M. *Social Control of Business*, 2d ed. New York: McGraw-Hill, 1939, pp. 95–96.

Colberg, Marshall R. "Minimum Wage Effects on Florida Economic Development." *Journal of Law and Economics*, October 1960.

—. "Property Rights and Motivation." *Proceedings and Reports.* Center for Yugoslav-American Studies, Research and Exchanges, The Florida State University, Vols. 12–13 (1978–1979), pp. 52–58.

Cowell, Alan. "Austerity Plan for Workers Is Approved in Germany." *The New York Times*, Saturday, June 29, 1996, pp. 17–18.

de Larosier, J. "Coexistence of Fiscal Deficits: High Tax Burdens in Consequence of Pressures for Public Spending." *IMF Survey*, March 22, 1982, p. 82.

de Tocqueville, Alexis. *Democracy in America.* Garden City, NY: Doubleday, 1969.

Demsētz, Harold. "Towards a Theory of Property Rights." *American Economic Review* (May 1967), pp. 347–359.

Dirlam, Joel B., and Alfred E. Kahn. *Fair Competition.* Ithaca, NY: Cornell University Press, 1954, Chapters 4 and 6.

Downs, Anthony. *An Economic Theory of Democracy.* New York: Harper, 1957.

—. *Inside Bureaucracy.* Boston: Little, Brown, 1967, Chapter 8.

Evans, Michael. "Bankruptcy of Keynesian Econometric Models." *Challenge* (January/February 1980), pp. 13–19.

Friedman, Milton. "Economic Sanctions," *Milton Friedman: Bright Promises Dismal Performance: An Economist's Protest.* William R. Allen (ed.). New York: Harcourt Brace Jovanovich, 1983, pp. 370–372.

—. "The Energy Crisis." *Milton Friedman: Bright Promises Dismal Performance: An Economist's Protest,* William R. Allen (ed.). New York: Harcourt Brace Jovanovich, 1983, pp. 141–152.

—, ed. *Essays in Positive Economics.* Chicago: University of Chicago Press, 1953.

—. "Government Revenue from Inflation." *Journal of Political Economy* (July/August 1971), pp. 852–854.

—. "A Monetary Theory of National Income." *Journal of Political Economy* (April/May 1971), pp. 323–337.

—. "Nobel Lecture: Inflation and Unemployment." *Journal of Political Economy* (June 1997), pp. 451–472.

—. "A Theoretical Framework for Monetary Analysis." *Journal of Political Economy* (April/May 1970), pp. 193–238.

—, and Anna J. Schwartz. *A Monetary History of the United States, 1867–1960.* Princeton, NJ: Princeton University Press for the National Bureau of Economic Research, 1963.

—, and Anna J. Schwartz. *Monetary Trends in the United States and United Kingdom: Their Relation to Income, Prices and Interest Rates 1867–1975.* Chicago: University of Chicago Press, 1982.

—, and Rose Friedman. *Free to Choose.* New York: Avon Books, 1981.

—, and Rose Friedman. *Tyranny of the Status Quo.* Orlando, FL: Harcourt, Brace Jovanovich, 1984.

Fromm, Gary, and Lawrence R. Klein. "A Comparison of Eleven Econometric Models of the United States." *American Economic Review* (May 1973), pp. 385–393.

Greenhouse, Linda. "Justices Grant U.S. Employers Tool to Bargain." *The New York Times*, Friday, June 21, 1996, p. A1.

Haberler, Gottfried. "Integration and Growth of the World Economy in Historical Perspective" *American Economic Review* (March 1964), pp. 1–22.

Hafer, R. W. "The Role of Fiscal Policy in the St. Louis Equation." *Review*, Federal Reserve Bank of St. Louis (January 1982), pp. 17–22.

Head, Simon. "The New, Restless Economy." *The New York Review,* February 29, 1996, pp. 47–52.

Hicks, John R. "The Keynes Centenary: A Skeptical Follower." *The Economist*, June 8, 1983, pp. 17–19.

Hirsch, Werner Z. *Law and Economics.* New York: Academic Press, 1979.

Hood, N., and S. Young. *The Economics of the Multi-National Enterprise.* New York: Longman, 1979.

Hoskins, W. Lee. "Defending Zero Inflation: All for Naught." *Quarterly Review* (Spring 1991), Federal Reserve Bank of Minneapolis, pp. 16–20.

Johnson, Harry. "The Ideology of Economic Policy in the New States." *Chicago Essays on Economic Development,* D. Wall (ed.). Chicago: University of Chicago Press, 1972, pp. 23–40.

Keeley, M. C., P. K. Robins, R. G. Spiegelman, and R. W. West. "The Labor Supply Effects and Costs of Alternative Negative Income Tax Programs." *Journal of Human Resources* (Winter 1978), Vol. 13, No. 1, pp. 3–36.

Klein, Lawrence R. "Commentary on the State of the Monetarist Debate." *Review,* Federal Reserve Bank of St. Louis (September 1973), pp. 9–12.

Levin, Harvey J. (ed.) *Business Organization and Public Policy.* New York: Rinehart, 1958.

Lewis, H. Gregg. *Unionism and Relative Wages in the United States.* Chicago: University of Chicago Press, 1963.

Macesich, George. "Are Wage Differentials Resilient? An Empirical Test." *Southern Economic Journal* (April 1961).

—. *Economic Nationalism and Stability.* Westport, CT: Praeger, 1995.

—. *Integration and Stabilization: A Monetary View.* Westport, CT: Praeger, 1996.

—. *The International Monetary Economy and the Third World.* New York: Praeger, 1981.

—. *Monetarism: Theory and Policy.* New York: Praeger, 1983.

—. *Monetary Policy and Politics.* Westport, CT: Praeger, 1992.

—. *Monetary Reform and Cooperation Theory.* New York: Praeger, 1989.

—. *Money and Democracy.* New York: Praeger, 1990.

—. *The Politics of Monetarism: Its Historical and Institutional Development.* Totowa, NJ: Rowman and Allanheld, 1984, pp. 16–38.

—. *Reform and Market Democracy.* New York: Praeger, 1991.

—. *Transformation and Emerging Markets.* Westport, CT: Praeger, 1996.

—, and Charles T. Stewart, Jr. "Recent Department of Labor Studies of Minimum Wage Effects." *Southern Economic Journal* (April 1960), pp. 281–290.

Marshall, Alfred. *Principles of Economics,* 8th ed. New York: Macmillan, 1920.

Monetary Policy Issues in the 1990s. A Symposium Sponsored by the Federal Reserve Bank of Kansas City, Jackson Hole, Wyoming, August 30–September 1, 1989. Kansas City: Federal Reserve Bank of Kansas City, 1989.

Mund, Vernon A. *Government and Business.* New York: Harper, 1955, Chapter 20.

Nutter, G. Warren. *The Extent of Enterprise Monopoly in the United States, 1899–1939.* Chicago: University of Chicago Press, 1951.

Passell, Peter. "Economic Scene." *The New York Times,* Thursday, June 6, 1996, p. C2.

—. "Economic Scene: Some Second Thoughts Arise on Benefits of Immigration." *The New York Times,* Thursday, July 4, 1996, p. C2.

Posner, Richard A. *Overcoming Law.* Cambridge: Harvard University Press, 1994.

Robinson, Joan. *The Economics of Imperfect Competition.* London: Macmillan, 1933.

Rohatyn, Felix. "World Capital: The Need and the Risks." *The New York Review of Books* (July 14, 1994), pp. 48–53.

Sanger, David E., and Steve Lohr. "A Search for Answers to Avoid the Layoffs." *The New York Times,* Saturday, March 9, 1996, p. 10.

Solo, Robert A. "The Neo-Marxist Theory of the State." *Journal of Economic Issues* (December 1978), Vol. 12, No. 4, pp. 829–842.

—. *The Positive State.* Cincinnati: South-Western Publishing Company, 1982, p. 57, 59.

Stein, H. *Fiscal Revolution in America.* Chicago: University of Chicago Press, 1969.

Stelzer, Irwin M. *Selected Antitrust Cases.* Homewood, IL: Irwin, 1955, Chapter 6.

Stigler, George J. "Competition in the United States." *Five Lectures in Economic Problems.* New York: Macmillan, 1950, pp. 46–65.

Watson, Donald S. "America's Power Plants." *The Economist,* Vol. 339, No. 7969, p. 82.

——. "Capitalism: Survey." *The Economist* (May 5, 1990), pp. 5–20.

——. "The C-Word Strikes Back." *The Economist,* Vol. 339, No. 7968, p. 76.

——. "Can the G7 Ride Again?" *The Economist,* Vol. 339, No. 7971, p. 76.

——. *Economic Policy.* Boston: Houghton Mifflin, 1960.

——. *The Economist,* June 24, 1995, pp. 3–22.

——. "Environmental Policy: Could Try Harder." *The Economist,* Vol. 337, No. 7937, p. 32–33.

——. "Of Beef, Bushes, and Bonds." *The Economist,* May 25, 1996, p. 84.

——. "Trade Unions." *The Economist,* Vol. 336, No. 7921, pp. 54–56.

——. "A Working Hypothesis." *The Economist,* Vol. 339, No. 7965, p. 74.

Index

About the Author

GEORGE MACESICH is Professor of Economics and Director of the Institute for Comparative Policy Studies at Florida State University. He is the author of many articles and books in the economics field, including eighteen with Praeger Publishers.

ISBN 0-275-95705-5

90000>

EAN

9 780275 957056

HARDCOVER BAR CODE